PARENTING TO IMPACT GENERATIONS

Dr. Ronald L. Bernier

© Copyright 2008 – Dr. Ronald L. Bernier

All rights reserved. This book is protected under the copyright laws of the United States of America. This book may not be copied or reprinted for commercial gain or profit. The use of short quotations or occasional page copying for personal or group study is permitted and encouraged. Permission will be granted upon request. Unless otherwise identified, Scripture quotations are from the New King James Version of the Bible.

Published by

Vision Publishing

Ramona, California

ISBN

978-1-61529-018-5

FOR INFORMATION ON ORDERING PLEASE CONTACT:

MASTER BUILDER MINISTRIES, INC.
397 Bay Street
Fall River, MA 02724
508-730-1735

PRINTED IN THE UNITED STATES OF AMERICA

Table of Contents

PARENTING TO IMPACT GENERATIONS 1

Table of Contents 3

Chapter 1 7

    Cultural Breakdown of Family Life 7

Chapter 2 15

    Raising Image Bearers 15

        Image Bearers 17

        Parenting is a privilege: 18

Children as Olive Plants 19

A Plant of Great Potential 20

Chapter 3 23

God's Basic Design for Family Life 23

Chapter 4 31

Respect for Authority 31

Why Should Children Honor Their Parents? 36

Today – Authority in Crisis 38

Chapter 5 41

Parental Authority 41

Jesus Illustrates the Dynamic of Personal Authority 43

Parental Authority – Derived from the Family 45

Parental Authority – Focused on Faith and Morality 47

Parental Authority – Aimed at the Child's Freedom 49

Parental Authority – Limited by the Child's Rights 50

Chapter 6 53

The Family in Community Life 53

Chapter 7 63

Managing Our Households 63

Chapter 8 71

Parental Obedience to God's Commands 71

Cultivating Obedience as our Primary Response 72

Choosing to Obey the Lord 73

Gaining a Conviction for Christian Education 74

Chapter 9 79

God's Law of Sowing and Reaping 79

Maintaining an Equal Yoke Between Parent and Teacher 81

Parents are Responsible for What is Taught their Child 83

An Ungodly Philosophy of Life Will Capture a Child's Mind 84

Children Should Be Taught About the Real World 86

God's Ultimate Purpose for Youth 87

Chapter 10 91

Growing in Our Obedience 91

Settling Your Alternatives within a Biblical Framework 91

The Equally Yoked Family 91

The Unequally Yoked Family 92

The Broken Home 94

How Long Should a Child Receive a Christian Education? 96

What about the Will of the Child? 98

Home School or Christian School? 100

Restoring the Parents as the Primary Educators 102

Chapter 1
Cultural Breakdown of Family Life

Many people believe that we are in the early stages of a post-Christian culture in America, just two generations behind Europe, which is now fully post-Christian. A big reason for this belief is the thinking of the current generation and their lack of any sense of moral absolutes. Hardly any adhere to the Christian faith, even in a nominal sense. This is not just in the culture at large; it is in our churches as well. It is estimated that we are loosing between 60-70% of our children from evangelical homes. The faith is not being picked up by the next generation. If you picture a relay race – not only is the baton being dropped – there is no one there to pick it up. The USA seems to be following the same post-Christian course as the rest of the declining West.

But this is not just a pattern in the West. As we move across mission fields all over the Two-Thirds World, it is very common that by the fourth generation whole movements of churches are producing a nominal generation of Christians. That means that the great-great grandchildren of those who came to Christ almost 100 years ago (in some areas representing thousands of new churches), are growing up without a real faith of their own. They are nominal – Christian in name only. The true faith is not being successfully passed on from generation to generation. One of the most crucial tasks for churches of each generation is to see that the faith is successfully passed on to the next generation. The biblical ideal is for the fourth generation to be stronger than the previous generations and to start a heritage that will bring blessings for many generations to come. Yet, this is often not the case.

One of the reasons that the church fails to pass on the faith successfully from generation to generation is that churches are not properly established in the elementary principles of God's Word (Heb. 6:1-2). One explanation is that we have become dull of hearing (Heb. 5:11-14). We have no modern day "catechism" to firmly establish an emerging generation in the elementary principles. We do not take seriously the training of parents in the awesome and critical task of "bringing their children up in the discipline and instruction of the Lord" (Eph. 6:4). This includes bringing up children in both behavior and belief. Most parents themselves are not trained in the elementary principles. Nor do they seem to seek or desire this training. After Martin Luther toured his country and realized the state of the churches (he even referred to the clergy as uneducated barbarians), he returned to his study and wrote his "little catechism" to begin the process of instructing fathers in how to lead their homes and train their children. We need to begin that same process in our homes today. If we expect to reverse the exodus of young adults from our churches, we must begin taking very seriously the importance of parents – especially fathers – in passing on the faith to their children.

We live in a culture where there is almost a complete breakdown of family life. The statistics are staggering. The divorce rate has more than tripled over the last few decades. The USA currently has the highest divorce rate in the world. Around 50% of today's teenagers are not living with both parents. These truly are the first stages of a post-Christian culture. We are producing a generation, even in our churches, of children who know little of the lifelong security and stability that comes from a mature, two-parent family, founded on the concept of life-long commitment and stable faith. A significant majority of our children are not continuing in the faith. Our churches are not that far behind culture. What can we do? How do we keep from experiencing the same breakdown as the families around us?

We will begin by examining a passage in 2 Timothy that describes what we should expect in the culture around us and that lays a foundation for how to build solid families. Rather than being lovers of God with our world revolving around God and our serving Him, we have replaced God with idolatry, which is simply misdirected love.

2 Timothy 3:1-17 (NKJV) [1] But know this, that in the last days perilous times will come: [2] For men will be lovers of themselves, lovers of money, boasters, proud, blasphemers, disobedient to parents, unthankful, unholy, [3] unloving, unforgiving, slanderers, without self-control, brutal, despisers of good, [4] traitors, headstrong, haughty, lovers of pleasure rather than lovers of God, [5] having a form of godliness but denying its power. And from such people turn away! [6] For of this sort are those who creep into households and make captives of gullible women loaded down with sins, led away by various lusts, [7] always learning and never able to come to the knowledge of the truth. [8] Now as Jannes and Jambres resisted Moses, so do these also resist the truth: men of corrupt minds, disapproved concerning the faith; [9] but they will progress no further, for their folly will be manifest to all, as theirs also was. [10] But you have carefully followed my doctrine, manner of life, purpose, faith, longsuffering, love, perseverance, [11] persecutions, afflictions, which happened to me at Antioch, at Iconium, at Lystra—what persecutions I endured. And out of *them* all the Lord delivered me. [12] Yes, and all who desire to live godly in Christ Jesus will suffer persecution. [13] But evil men and impostors will grow worse and worse, deceiving and being deceived. [14] But you must continue in the things which you have learned and been assured of, knowing from whom you have learned *them,* [15] and that from childhood you have known the Holy Scriptures, which are able to make you wise for salvation through faith which is in Christ Jesus. [16] All Scripture *is* given by inspiration of God, and *is* profitable for doctrine, for reproof, for correction, for instruction in righteousness, [17] that the man of God may be complete, thoroughly equipped for every good work.

Reflecting on 2 Timothy 3:1-17, we must remember that this passage is in the context of the Pastoral Epistles. Paul wrote to Timothy and Titus to give them instructions on how to fully establish churches and how to keep them on course over the long haul. The specific context of 2 Timothy is a challenge to Timothy to keep the faith and to find other faithful men to whom he could entrust the sound doctrine for the next generation (2 Tim. 2:1-2). In 2 Timothy 3, Paul describes the culture during the last days. In this message we are particularly interested in what he says about the breakdown of the family. The lack of respect and honor is one characteristic of a generation marked by disobedience to parents. Also noted are households where men entered and led weak wives astray. They deceptively tried to keep these women dependent on them and what they said. Added to this are a whole set of individual characteristics that mark a culture driven by rampant individualism – a culture that is selfish, driven by money (yet no work ethic), lacking personal disciplines and controls (no standard of discipline), destroying lives of others (usually for their own personal gain), always seeking personal pleasure – whatever feels good. This has become a mirror of our culture – the breakdown of the family in the wake of unbridled pursuits of individual interest and pleasures.

This whole section of Scripture is followed by a prediction, in 2 Timothy 4:1-4. That many will fall into the ways of the culture and not listen (even close their eyes) to sound doctrine – the teaching of elementary principles. Not only will they fall into the ways of the culture, but they will find teachers who will adapt the message to the culture, who will twist the principles into what they want to hear. The most "successful" teachers, those who gain the largest response of the culture, will have to tell people what they want to hear. In other words they will compromise the truth because others will not listen to sound doctrine. In fact it will be the popularity poll that will determine what truth is. They will have to water down the message or change the principles. That is why Paul warned Timothy in 1 Tim. 6:6, to "preach and teach these principles." It is imperative not to compromise. In 2 Timothy 4:2, he was to preach the word "in season and out."

As you read through 2 Timothy 3:1-17 it is important to think through the following questions:

- What traits will characterize culture in "the last days"?
- Which of those traits directly relate to the breakdown of the family?
- What was key(s) in Timothy's life that kept him strong?
- What does the passage teach us about stopping the breakdown of our own families?

The apostle Paul commented that "in the last days perilous times will come." This is a description of a recurring reality for all Christians in all times and places. There would be times of stress, from the time of Paul to our present day and into the future! Later in this chapter (2 Timothy 3), Paul insists that all who follow Jesus will suffer persecution (3:12), as Jesus Himself had warned (John 15:18-20). This raises a very troubling question for me. Why are Christians in America so comfortable? Why are we so accepted and well-received? Only two things must be true. Either we live in a Christian culture that naturally provides a climate of acceptance and support, or we have accommodated ourselves to the values established by our non-Christian culture. I don't find enough evidence to convince me that ours is a Christian culture. Our comfort and acceptance can only suggest to me that we have been tamed by the world around us and have acquiesced with the world's values much more that we realize or dare admit.

This becomes quite evident as Paul describes the roots of trouble and perilous times in verses 2-5. The reasons that Christians will be persecuted in troubled times grow out of the distorted values of people around and among them. Paul list 20 characteristics of people who often unintentionally create a climate of trouble for those who would take Jesus seriously. We can narrow this list to 3 types of love:

- Lovers of themselves
- Lovers of money
- Lovers of pleasure

Now let's turn our attention to the faith of our children. What does this section teach us about the fate of our children in this type of culture? First, they are part of a generation that is much like the one in this passage. Most individuals in this kind of generation will not respond to sound doctrine. They will not accept the teaching and build their lives around the first principles. So our children who do will be in the minority; it will take exceptional strength to build their lives upon the teaching.

Second, they need to be taught the elementary principles of the faith from childhood, as Timothy was (3:15). Timothy's tradition ran deep. He learned his faith from his mother, Eunice and his grandmother, Lois (2 Tim. 1:5). Then Paul came along, evidently when Timothy was in his teens, and took him under his wing. If there is no pipeline of the transfer of our faith to our children, there will be no harvest in the teen years.

Third, our children need to be challenged to continue in the faith (3:14). Even though Timothy was a young leader, he needed to be challenged to continue in the teaching. The temptation was there, even with Timothy, to be affected by the culture and fail to continue in the faith. Sometimes, as parents, this is where we let down our guard and fail to challenge our children to continue. You can see how difficult it is to keep the faith alive and developing from generation to generation.

We can see three generations here: Timothy's grandmother Lois, his mother Eunice, and Timothy. Paul reached back into Timothy's spiritual roots, his childhood, and set the learning of the Scriptures at the core of his ability to continue with the faith. He learned the Scriptures within the context of his family. As a spiritual mentor to Timothy, Paul simply built upon the foundation that was laid by his family. If we expect to reverse the exodus of children from our churches and eventually build strong, multiplying churches, we have to build the Scriptures into the lives of our children from childhood.

Fran Sciacca wrote the following except in *"Generation at Risk: What Legacy Are the Baby-Boomers Leaving Their Kids"*:

> "We may doubt that we can reclaim an entire generation; however, we certainly can reclaim our own children and their friends. The home is the reasonable starting place for healing the church. And the most effective and lasting instrument for accomplishing this healing is parental example. We as parents need to take serious inventory of our own spiritual lives. Do we have a distinctly biblical worldview? [In other words, do we live out a Biblical lifestyle based on what we believe from Scripture or is our lifestyle mixed?] Do we measure our behavior by the standards of Scripture or by the guy next door? Do our children hear us talk about God in a real and personal way, or do they perceive from our conversations that our faith is an impersonal subject to be studied? Are we living out our faith before them as authentic aliens or simply as tourists?"

> "We must ask ourselves other questions. Do our children see us spending time with God in prayer and Bible study or do they merely see us rushing from one religious activity to another? Have our children ever felt the liberty to ask us tough questions about God's existence, the truth of Christianity, and the future of man? [Would we have an answer?] Do our children see us laboring to enlarge the kingdom of God, or seeking to enhance

our own kingdoms? Do our children see us collecting "things," or investing in people? Do they believe they have an option?'

"These are not merely provocative questions. They are penetrating queries into our own spiritual lives, asked of the ones who know us best. I encourage every parent of junior- or senior-high children to spend a half day with your kids privately; ask them these questions about yourself. Assure them that you will not hold them "hostage" to their answers; give them the liberty to be honest. They'll tell you what they "see," which incidentally is also what they are going to become someday. [For those who are not parents or are unmarried, this suggestion fits just as well. Simply asks your questions of those who know you best.]"

The personal investment and sacrifice required to cultivate a biblical worldview and lifestyle are enormous, but the stakes are high. An entire generation is at risk! Our lives are on the line, and so is the future of the church.

As you consider this chapter, you might want to apply what you have learned by exploring additional questions:

- How can you encourage your children and grandchildren to fully embrace the faith?

- If you don't have children, how can you encourage young adults in your church to fully embrace the faith?

- If you are a young adult yourself, evaluate the likelihood that you will fully embrace the faith when you are completely on your own.

- How can you personally make a positive impact on this issue?

Chapter 2
Raising Image Bearers

An elderly gentleman strolling through a quiet residential neighborhood came upon a little boy sitting on the curb crying. "What's the trouble, son" he asked. "Are you lost?" "Worse than that," the youngster sobbed. "Mom's book on child-raising is lost, and now she's using her own judgment!"

We live in a society where we have lost the book on child raising and are living out the consequences of using our own judgment. The book of Judges calls this "everyone was doing what was right in their own eyes." The result is that the behavior of children has dramatically changed. In 1940 the top offenses committed by public school students were: talking, chewing gum, making noise, running in halls, getting out of turn in line, wearing improper clothing and not putting paper in the wastebasket. Today, the top offenses have changed to: rape, robbery, assault, burglary, arson, bombing, murder, substance abuse, sexual abuse, gang warfare, occult practices and suicide. Today's children live in a different world from the one you and I remember.

The nuclear family has exploded. Families are fragmented. Today's projections indicate that 2 out of 3 white children between birth and 18 will spend at least part of their growing-up years in a single-parent family. In the black community, 19 out of 20 children are expected to do so. Several years ago, the University of California tested 5th and 6th graders to determine what caused them the highest degree of sadness, anxiety, and depression. The top answers? Having parents separate or divorce. Having parents argue with one another, and having parents who didn't spend enough time with them.

Time Magazine reported the findings of a certain study measuring the long-term effects of growing up in a fragmented family. The Time article concluded that close to half of the children from families broken by divorce go into adulthood as men and women who worry, are underachievers, have poor self-images, and often are very angry. Two thirds of the girls, many of whom had seemingly sailed through the crisis of divorce, suddenly became deeply anxious as young adults, unable to make lasting commitments and fearful of betrayal in intimate relationships. Many boys, who were more overly troubled in the post divorce years, failed to develop a sense of independence, confidence or purpose. They drifted in and out of college and from job to job.

Another reason for the changing behavior of children is the increased pressure imposed by overachieving parents. Either they are preoccupied with their own careers or they put the same kind of pressure to succeed on their children. It's a "toddler-eat-toddler" world out there. Not only do we have Yuppies now we have "Yuppie Puppies" competing for the honor roll in pre-school classes. Socrates said, "Could I climb to the highest place in Athens, I would lift my voice and proclaim: 'Fellow citizens, why do ye turn and scrape every stone to gather wealth and take so little care of your own children to whom one day you must relinquish it all?"

A third reason for changing childhood behavior is the role models children are exposed to today. Eddie Haskel looks like an altar boy compared to current media characters.

Numerous other factors negatively influence children's behavior. Peer pressure, drugs and alcohol, pornography, nuclear threat, economic and environmental instability, increased sexual abuse, sexual permissiveness, domestic violence and AIDS. Suicide for teenagers has tripled in the last 30 years. Four-hundred thousand teens attempt suicide each year and 6000 succeed.

We are called to stand firm in a changing world. We must learn to instill in our children strength, integrity, and values that will help them to stand in a changing world. Newly married couples should devote themselves to solidifying their marriages before they even consider having children. Nearly 34 % of divorces occur within 4 years of the wedding. Marriage is not something one tries on for size, and then decides whether to keep; rather it is something one decides with a promise and then bends every effort to keep. It takes time to develop communication skills and the ability to solve conflicts and build the security that leads to intimacy.

The time to build some of these skills is when a couple begins to court. It takes time and effort to get on track spiritually and sort out our values and priorities. Many young people do not even consider these things before beginning relationships. Often times these young people need healing from the past. Without this healing they pass on broken batons to another generation.

Malachi challenged the casual view of marriage that people had in his day by reminding them that God ordained marriage. He goes on to say that one of the reasons for which God ordained marriage was so that godly offspring might be raised (Mal. 2:13-16). The apostle Paul spoke of marriage and children; he said he wanted the younger widows to remarry and bear children (1 Tim. 5:14). In another place, he states that young women are to be encouraged (or taught) to love their husbands and their children (Titus 2:4).

In a recent poll, 1500 mall shoppers were asked what they wished for most when they blow out their birthday candles. Men and women gave vastly different answers. The number one wish of women was "more time with spouse." Among the men, that wish came in at 27th on the list. What did the guys wish for most often? A lower golf score!

Image Bearers

God created Adam and Eve in His own image and pronounced them 'very good!' Then He commanded them to make additional reproductions of His image through procreation. Adam and Eve's multiplied offspring were to brighten the world by mirroring the greatness of God's character and power.

The primary reason for having children is to raise shining, active, young image-bearers who are motivated and trained to carry the torch of authentic Christianity into the next generation. This commission goes beyond just the parent; but to the entire church as the community of oneness that God created is commissioned as well. Adam and Eve were to expand the community of oneness. This was not an individual command, but a community command. They were given both a Dominion and a Domestic mandate. Adam and Eve's disobedience stained not only themselves, but their lineage as well. From that day on, parents would birth children who had the potential to reflect God's glory, but drawing out that potential would require great amounts of parental leadership, love, energy, interaction, discipline, and prayer.

All of us who truly understand the goal of raising children – to draw out the image-bearing potential of each child – to build a community where that potential can be utilized and encouraged – must become fully engaged in the challenge. We can no longer just build businesses. We must build character, value, and vision into young lives. For those of you who are parents – see this season of parenting as the ultimate spiritual challenge, worthy of your best efforts, fervent prayers, and the largest investments of time. For those of you who are not parents – you must get a corporate vision of the church as the bride of Christ and her responsibility to raise godly offspring. You, too, must invest your best efforts. Raising godly offspring demands that we impart life – emotional, spiritual and physical. We can't impart what we don't have.

Parenting is a privilege:

Psalm 128:1-6 (NKJV) [1] A Song of Ascents. Blessed *is* everyone who fears the LORD, Who walks in His ways. ² When you eat the labor of your hands, You *shall be* happy, and *it shall be* well with you. ³ Your wife *shall be* like a fruitful vine In the very heart of your house, **Your children like olive plants All around your table.** ⁴ Behold, thus shall the man be blessed Who fears the LORD. ⁵ The LORD bless you out of Zion, And may you see the good of Jerusalem All the days of your life. ⁶ Yes, may you see your children's children. Peace *be* upon Israel!

Psalm 127:3-5 (NKJV) ³ **Behold, children *are* a heritage from the LORD,** The fruit of the womb *is* a reward. ⁴ Like arrows in the hand of a warrior, So *are* the children of one's youth. ⁵ Happy *is* the man who has his quiver full of them; They shall not be ashamed, But shall speak with their enemies in the gate.

Children as Olive Plants

What exactly does the olive-plant picture mean? It implies that we should have a high regard for our children. The olive tree was the most important tree in Palestine. It is depicted as the king of the trees (Jud. 9:8-9). It is dignified by comparing God's people to an olive tree planted by God (Rom. 11:17). Scripture exalts this tree by specifically prescribing that the oil of the olive tree – and only that oil – be used to consecrate the priests and fuel the lamps in the tabernacle (Exod. 27:20; 30:22-33).

Consider the foolish virgins (Matt. 25:1-13) who "took their lamps and took no oil with them." In their watching, were they considering the next generation? Or were they just concerned with themselves being taken up? In other words – children are valuable and precious.

Jesus felt the same way. He knew all about children. He knew that they were born sinners and therefore needed to be regenerated and redeemed (Psalm 51:3-5; 58:3). Jesus was fully aware that they needed to be changed by God's grace (Eph. 2:1-8). He had no unrealistic ideals about perfection or innocence (Prov. 22:15). Yet He evidenced a high regard for them. He sternly rebuked His disciples for trying to prevent certain parents from bringing their children to Him (Mark 10:13-16).

Like Jesus, we must be realistic in our attitudes toward children. We must realize that our children have the potential for great wickedness (Psalm 51:5; 58:3). They are born sinners and must be regenerated by God's Spirit and redeemed by God's grace. Our children need God's forgiveness for their sins. They need His help to become truly worthwhile, God-honoring, olive plant persons. Without Him, they cannot bear fruit for God (John 15:1-6).

Biblical realism requires us to see our children as persons of great value and worth, despite their needs and deficiencies. Our children should be important to us not because they are ours, but because they are persons made in God's image and are God's gifts to us.

A Plant of Great Potential

There are numerous ways in which the olive plant and its fruit were used. Olives and olive oil were used for food (Deut. 24:20), illumination (Lev. 24:2), consecrating religious workers (Exod. 3:22-33), cosmetic purposes (Ruth 3:3), medicinal and hygienic functions (Luke 10:34), religious ceremonies (Gen. 28:28), and even as a commodity of exchange (1 Kings 5:11; Luke 16:6).

In addition, the olive tree and its fruit are symbols of joy, prosperity, and peace.

> **Isaiah 61:3** (NKJV) [3] To console those who mourn in Zion, To give them beauty for ashes, The oil of joy for mourning, The garment of praise for the spirit of heaviness; That they may be called trees of righteousness, The planting of the LORD, that He may be glorified."

> **Psalm 45:7** (NKJV) ⁷ You love righteousness and hate wickedness; Therefore God, Your God, has anointed You With the oil of gladness more than Your companions.

The tree itself was noted for its beauty (Jer. 11:16; Hos. 14:6). It's wood was valuable for fuel and construction purposes (1 Kings 6:23, 31-33). When the olive crop failed, it was considered a national tragedy (Hab. 3:7).

What does this suggest about children? We should have high expectations for them. Our expectations need to be in keeping with their personal giftings and stage development, but mustn't underestimate their God-given capacities. Olive plants need careful attention to bear fruit. The soil around them must frequently be plowed. They need water and fertilizer. They thrive best in warm and sunny situations.

Children need diligent care. We must bring them up in the instruction and discipline of the Lord (Eph. 6:4). We must be diligent in teaching them God's Word in structured and spontaneous situations. We must be genuinely and attractively spiritual in our own lifestyle. We must hide God's Word in our own hearts, making our entire lives living epistles to our children of God's truth. We must provide an environment that is conductive to the development of godly character and conduct. We must seek to eliminate from ourselves and our homes anything that will inhibit fruitfulness. We can't bear fruit for our children – the olive tree must bear its own fruit. We must teach our children to accept responsibility. But we can't be guilty of excessive pushing and shoving.

Our children are plants not branches. A plant has an independent existence. A branch is simply part of a tree. We are to respect the individuality of our children. God didn't intend them to be carbon copies of us.

We must provide the tools, the encouragement, the example, and the structure for our children to bear fruit. We want to develop in our children an inner motivation and self-control – the ability to think, choose, and live biblically without the need for excessive external motivation or control. Provide them with fences not straightjackets.

Our goal is to help children grow to be interdependently dependent on Christ and His Word. The children are to be plants within a larger olive orchard and olive plants around our table. Ultimately, we want to point them away from ourselves to Christ as the One upon whom they are most dependent. We want them to grow into a mature relationship with us and not a dependent relationship.

Our children as olive plants around our table convey the idea of fellowship and loyalty. It suggests that building our family God's way involves developing family cohesiveness and togetherness. This is our foundational service arm to our community.

Chapter 3

God's Basic Design for Family Life

> **Ephesians 6:1-4** (NKJV) [1] Children, obey your parents in the Lord, for this is right. [2] *"Honor your father and mother,"* which is the first commandment with promise: [3] *"that it may be well with you and you may live long on the earth."* [4] And you, fathers, do not provoke your children to wrath, but bring them up in the training and admonition of the Lord.
>
> **Colossians 3:20-21** (NKJV) [20] Children, obey your parents in all things, for this is well pleasing to the Lord. [21] Fathers, do not provoke your children, lest they become discouraged.

The basic design for the family is very simple. There are a couple of guidelines for children and one main guideline for fathers that, when properly understood, incorporate the role of both the father and the mother. The purpose of the literary form that Paul used was to express the ideal household (family) and the ideal city (community life). This passage (Ephesians 5:22-6:9), along with Colossians 3:18-4:1, 1 Peter 2:13-3:7, and large portions of 1 Timothy and Titus, sets forth the elementary principles of life in a believing family and life in the family of God – a local church. We are going to focus in on family life, especially the relationship between parents and children.

Paul first addresses children. Several observations can be made from the very first line. First, Paul chooses a word for children that clearly includes older children as well as younger. There are two forms of the Greek word for children. The word in this text is the Greek word *"teknon"*. It refers to all children. When you want to refer to small children you insert an "i" into the word – *"teknion"*. Why is this important? Because these instructions are for all children, not just the little ones. Second, these children are to obey their parents. This means that they are to place themselves under their parents as authority in their lives. Third, they are to obey both parents, not just the father, who is addressed in Ephesians 6:4. Fourth, they are to obey their parents "in the Lord." That is, since the children are Christians, they are to live that way, regardless of how godly their parents are. The same idea is found in the next section, 6:5-9, where slaves are to obey their masters as if they were obeying and serving Christ. This idea of obeying carries the concept of serving one's parents. And it carries the spirit of the child as well – a spirit marked by a desire to please Christ. Fifth, the direction is given to children because it is right.

These simple observations really set only one thing in place – authority. Notice that children are responsible to place themselves under the authority of their parents. The word obey is a very simple yet graphic Greek term, *hupakouo*, a compound word from *akouo*, "to hear," and the preposition *hupo*, which means "under." So the Holy Spirit is saying, "Children, get under the authority of your parents and listen." In contradiction, the society we live in says we need to liberate children, free them from parental authority. A child must have the right to choose his own destiny, his own religion, his own thoughts, and his own perspective on economics or morality or whatever, they say. But the Bible says quite the contrary. Children are to get under the authority of their parents and listen to them. That is God's pattern and design for the family. Since the directive is given to believing children, it must refer to children who are old enough to be believers and who start removing themselves from the authority of their parents, probably adolescents and young adults. Though it is not clear at what age that authority changes to honor (next verse), the authority would clearly cover the time that they reside in their father's household.

The responsibility of children is extended in Ephesians 6:2-3. The command to obey (authority) shifts to honor as the children go out and establish their own households. Notice that this responsibility to honor is life-long and includes both parents. This includes the responsibility for caring for the aged and widowed parents.

After addressing the children, Paul turned to address the parents. We know that both parents are in view because Ephesians 6:1-2 states that children are to obey and honor their parents. So why then did Paul just address fathers? Because fathers are to take the lead in the training and discipline of the children. The father carries an element of authority just by the nature of being the man, while the mother has more of a nurturing aspect by her nature of being a woman. This shows how important the father's role is on one hand or how destructive his absence would be on the other hand. Specifically, the parent's responsibility, led by the father, is to pass on the faith to his children. This involves two elements – discipline and instruction.

Two specific words are used by Paul to describe the training process: "discipline and instruction." The first word "discipline" (literally *'paideia,'* a common word used even today for good overall education) referred, in Paul's day, to the general upbringing attained by discipline. The word "instruction" literally means "to place in mind", along with the admonition to follow the teaching. The admonition seems to cover the entire training process. However, the sphere is narrowed to the discipline and instruction "of the Lord.' The context calls forth the idea of the parents teaching in a disciplined manner, with the father clearly seeing to it, so that the children's lives are shaped around the elementary principles of the faith. This issue is not whether parents home school their children or send them to Christian schools, but whether the parents, overseen by the father, are shaping the entire education process around the faith. He needs to see that they are fully trained in the faith, and that they embrace it.

In the Colossians 3:20-21 text, we see that the family is to be a center for caring, caring for persons who are seen as unique and precious, all the recipients of Christ's love. The family as a center for caring makes it the place we can go and be when all other doors are shut. Because we care, we notice. Because we care, we listen. Because we care, we are honest. Because we care, we share. These are the things that enable us to grow. Discipline may become a harsh system which provokes and discourages children. Paul is aware of this, so he cautioned children and fathers. Obedience is the key word. But we must see obedience in the context of the all-pervading love of God. We trust God and can obey Him because we know He wills our ultimate good. As parents we may be able to demand obedience from our children (but that will be short lived unless our children can trust us), and what will happen to them in the process will be detrimental, even destructive, unless they are assured that we are committed to their ultimate well-being. Parent's relationships with children shape their personality and especially influence how they relate to themselves and others.

In this Colossians passage to fathers, Paul adds one additional insight to his instructions. He tells fathers not to exasperate their children. The word literally means "to stir up or provoke a person to the point that they become embittered." It pictures completely frustrating a son or daughter. Maybe that's because their father is too demanding. Maybe he's over corrective. In the worst case, it refers to fathers who are abusive. The clear result: the children lose heart and give up. The word here literally means "to become discouraged or to lose all motivation." This state of being disheartened may become anger and rebellion or turn inward and become depression and lack of purpose and direction. Regardless of the outcome, a father who exasperates his children fails to properly pass on the faith to his children, and probably will lead them toward rejecting the faith. The absence of fathers is one reason for children leaving the faith. Another clear reason, from this passage, is fathers who are too harsh or demanding with their children.

The directive actually implies several things about shaping the lives of children in a way that causes them to embrace the faith. First, it assumes that children desire to please their fathers. Otherwise, it would be almost impossible to exasperate them. It also infers that fathers, who are naturally the authority figures, are prone to overuse that authority, which is often referred to as being authoritarian. It also infers that fathers are not to avoid the use of authority, since children are to be obedient to their parents. In other worlds, they should not be too permissive either. Authority is critical to shaping the lives of children, but it must be used to shape their lives around the faith – "to bring them up in the discipline and instruction of the Lord" (Ephesians 6:4).

Many today believe that children who are pretty much left on their own will grow up just fine. Yet, Scripture is clear that authority is needed in the process. Boundaries must be set to shape their lives correctly. Eventually children have to make their own choices as to whether they will continue in the faith. Nevertheless, as parents, especially fathers, we are commanded to guide and shape their lives in a way that encourages and develops their faith. Fathers are not to be authoritarian or permissive, but rather authoritative.

Notice that mothers are not given the same warning. Why? 1 Thessalonians 2:7, 11, tells us that mothers are more naturally nurturing and fathers are more exhortive and challenging.

Shaping the lives of their children is clearly the parent's responsibility. It demands a clear line of authority in the home, with parents' authority securely in place. The absence of clear lines of authority with their children, or the absence of a balanced use of authority, being too harsh or demanding, is at the core of why children are not continuing in the faith.

How do we as parents make our children angry, provoke them to open rebellion or cause them to smolder in anger? Here is a list of potential problems:

- **Overprotection.** This occurs when you smother your children, fence them in, never trust them, and always question whether they are really telling you the truth. Never give them an opportunity to develop independence. In their environment, where everyone else takes certain risks and has certain opportunities, if they are compressed into a very confined area they will begin to resent you. Children are people, and little by little they need to face the world and learn how to deal with it.

- **Favoritism.** Isaac favored Esau over Jacob, and Rebekah favored Jacob over Esau: what terrible agony that caused! Don't ever compare your children with each other. You can discourage a child, make him angry, and break his spirit by doing that. Comments like, "Why can't you get good grades like your sister" or "I never have to tell your brother twice to do anything" can destroy a child.

- **Pushing for achievement.** You can push your child so hard that the child will have absolutely no sense of fulfillment – nothing he does will ever be enough. Many parents pressure their children to excel in school, sports, or other activities, and it causes them to become bitter.

- **Discouragement.** You can provoke a child to anger by discouraging him, always withholding your approval and only telling him what is wrong with him. I believe that for every time you tell your child he had done something wrong you ought to equalize it by telling him something he has done properly. Sometimes you may have to look hard, and you may have to be creative, but find something for which to praise him. A child responds to approval and encouragement just like you do!

- **Failure to sacrifice.** Make your children feel like they are an intrusion on your life, and that will provoke them to anger. Tell someone "well, we'd love to go with you, but we've got these kids, and we can't get anybody to stay with them. It's this way all the time!" Does that sound familiar? Make your children feel unwanted, make them feel like they are always in the way, and deep inside, resentment will begin to build.

- **Failure to allow for childishness.** Some parents make sure that if the children do anything that is not mature and intellectual, they are put down for it. Children will say silly things, and suggest silly ideas. But it should be exciting just to let them say what they want, even if it is absurd. If you have to laugh, laugh later, not then. Let them grow. Don't condemn them for being children!

- **Neglect.** David neglected Absalom, and Absalom became the greatest heartbreak of David's life. You cannot neglect your children and win! Be there and be available to share your lives with them. You can't afford the price of being too busy for your children!

- **Withdrawing love.** Never use your love as a punishment, or even as a threat. "Daddy won't like you if you do that!" Is that how God deals with us? Of course not!

- **Cruel words and punishment.** Be careful; those are fragile little lives you're dealing with. Fathers, don't push your weight around or use your superior strength against your children. They can be battered not only physically but also devastated verbally. Parents are more sophisticated, so they can be more sarcastic than children, but you can destroy the heart of a child by your verbal barrage. I'm always amazed that we say things to our children we would never say to any other human being. We would be afraid it would ruin our relationship and reputation!

How does your family line up with the Biblical guidelines found in

Ephesians 6:1-4? Colossians 3:20-21? Reflect on the state of your family? Is your family in line with Christ's design? If not, where do you need to make changes? Are they major? Have clear lines of authority been established within your household? Are you loving and patient with your children as you train and discipline them? Are your children discouraged or giving up on their relationship with you?

As a young adult, think about your relationship with your parents? How did they raise you? Or how are they raising you if you are still in the home? How do you think you will likely go about training your children in the future?

If you are a single parent, how can you compensate for the imbalance, since both parents are not present?

If a grandparent, how can you contribute to helping your children raise their children in a balanced manner?

If you are not a parent, how can you contribute to other's children through your influence?

Chapter 4
Respect for Authority

Exodus 20:12 (NKJV) [12] "Honor your father and your mother, that your days may be long upon the land which the LORD your God is giving you.

Deuteronomy 5:16 (NKJV) [16] 'Honor your father and your mother, as the LORD your God has commanded you, that your days may be long, and that it may be well with you in the land which the LORD your God is giving you.

Ephesians 6:1-4 (NKJV) [1] Children, obey your parents in the Lord, for this is right. [2] *"Honor your father and mother,"* which is the first commandment with promise: [3] *"that it may be well with you and you may live long on the earth."* [4] And you, fathers, do not provoke your children to wrath, but bring them up in the training and admonition of the Lord.

There is a stubborn single-mindedness to the Fifth Commandment. To get a feel for the sharpness of its focus, we may notice a couple of things that it does not say. First, the commandment ignores the warm affection all parents want from their children. It does not tell children to feel happy about their parents; it does not tell us to like being with parents on camping trips or to relish having them over for dinner; it does not encourage happy emotional relationships. All that it commands is honor.

Secondly, the command does not tell parents to honor their children. The child's own right to respect is not in view. We might agree that children deserve a sort of honor as precious human beings, but this commandment is not about their worth as individuals. It is concerned with family structure and the role of parents as teachers and leaders in the family.

The ancient word for honor was something like "weightiness" (Hebrew, *kabad*). To honor persons you had to respect them as people who carried a great deal of weight in your life. That is, you had to let them have influence, dignity, and above all authority for you. The Hebrew word *"kabad"* smacks a little more of the military academy than dinner at home on Mother's Day. It is an ordering term for great strength.

A child who honored his parents fits naturally into the ancient Hebrew family. The Hebrew clan clustered around a patriarchal center. The oldest living male was the hub around which the family wheel turned; and the family included great-grandchildren, grandchildren, children, along with an assortment of servants, slaves, and concubines. Children were neither a nuisance nor an emotional luxury, but part of productive teams. Each one contributed to the welfare of the family. They helped keep back the ravages of nature and helped the family make a go of the farm. And, above all, they were the next chapter in God's romance with the human family, the link between God's covenant of the past and His salvation in the future.

A child was rewarded by getting his selfhood from his family. Today so many children are trying to find themselves both young and old. In the Hebrew culture a child was not merely an individual named Pete or Tom, but was identified by his parent's name, Levi-son-of-Ashur. The child was secure in his historical roots and propelled into the future by God's prophetic promises. Moreover, children were accustomed to living with an autocrat of a father, whom they saw as clan ruler, warrior, high priest, and judge, as well as father. We can understand why young Hebrews did not resent the Fifth Commandment as a bridle on their galloping individuality. And remember that the sons who heard the commandment were often themselves men who had become warriors, rulers, priests, and fathers.

But if we can see that honoring parents came more or less naturally for Hebrew children, this does not tell us what a Hebrew child was expected to do by way of honoring parents. The writers of the Old Testament could spot outrageous acts of dishonor more easily than they could define honor. When they did indicate flagrant violations of a parents' honor they recommended no mercy.

> **Exodus 21:15, 17** (NKJV) [15] "And he who strikes his father or his mother shall surely be put to death…[17] "And he who curses his father or his mother shall surely be put to death.

We hardly need to be told, of course, that it is dishonor to curse or cuff your parents. But what is worth noticing is that this was not just a private family affair; it was a social offense calling for community response (Deut. 21:18-21). The health of the entire community was at stake. If one was willing to bring an heir to the elders of the community – He was just as willing to see justice on other delinquents.

No wonder, then, that when a child ignores the "weightiness" of a parent, "all Israel shall hear, and fear" (Deut. 21:21). Dishonor a parent, and you remove a pillar from the foundations of Israel's society. This basis for honor would affect all other institutions.

But what did this deference and respect for parents come down to? Honor was a willingness at least to listen to the voice of one's father or mother, those who God gives to be our teachers and guides. For Israel, the family was the school where a person learned who he was and what God expected him to do. Life's basic questions were answered: Who am I? Where did I come from? For what purpose was I born?

> **Deuteronomy 6:6-8** (NKJV) [6] "And these words which I command you today shall be in your heart. [7] You shall teach them diligently to your children, and shall talk of them when you sit in your house, when you walk by the way, when you lie down, and when

you rise up. ⁸ You shall bind them as a sign on your hand, and they shall be as frontlets between your eyes.

In and through the family the good word was passed to all generations of the human race; and in the family the father was designated spokesman:

> **Psalm 78:5** (NKJV) ⁵ For He established a testimony in Jacob, And appointed a law in Israel, Which He commanded our fathers, That they should make them known to their children;

The father's authorized role was family storyteller; the child's authentic role was to be a listener. He showed his respect for the father by listening with a mind bent toward believing and obeying. In the long run the father's honor rested with the integrity of his office as spokesman for God in the family, the teller of God's story and the teacher of God's law. And the honor a child gave him was wrapped up primarily in his respect for his father's office.

A child honored his parents long after their roles were reversed. When the parent grew weak and the child grew strong, when the child became the parents' caregiver, when the parents' economic value was small and the child's was great (Lev. 27:7), the child remained a child called to honor his parents. The parents were to be kept at center stage in family affairs: They were never to be begrudged space, never to be asked to leave home.

> **Proverbs 19:26** (NKJV) ²⁶ He who mistreats *his* father *and* chases away *his* mother *Is* a son who causes shame and brings reproach.

The power of parents might wane and their active authority diminish, but they always stand for God before the child, and they never lose their dignity as caretakers and teachers. Today more than at any other time in our culture we are more concerned with our own individual happiness than with our duties and responsibilities. We should embrace our responsibilities and not begrudge them.

Israel's family life is a profile of how the divine commandment infiltrated ancient Jewish ways. From it we can extract something of what the Lord meant for families across the borders of time and culture. What we distill is an unsentimental notion of honor, not the platitudes of the typical Mother's Day card, but moral commitment to filial respect and long-term loyalty.

Paul's uncomplicated word to Christian children carried on the Hebrew expectation:

> **Colossians 3:20** (NKJV) [20] Children, obey your parents in all things, for this is well pleasing to the Lord.
>
> **Ephesians 6:1** (NKJV) [1] Children, obey your parents in the Lord, for this is right.

Here is a somber way to honor one's parents. A hug or a kiss on the cheek is very pleasant, but nothing suits honor better than doing what your father or mother tells you to do. Paul's word is, of course, meant for young children, not the child-adults who need to find other ways of honor beyond obedience. Obedience is not the be-all and end-all of honor, but honor for parents, like honor to God, begins with obedience and lacking it comes to nothing.

> **James 1:26** (NKJV) [26] If anyone among you thinks he is religious, and does not bridle his tongue but deceives his own heart, this one's religion *is* useless.

The scattered biblical data gives us some hints of what honoring a parent meant. A child was early led to understand that he was brought into life and was to find his own identity as a member of a family, not as a mere individual. He knew that he was not an equal in the family alliance but was expected to defer to his parents as go-betweens between himself and God, mediators of his own past and pointers to his future. He accepted them as his teachers and guides, as well as his trusted protectors and nourishers. When he listened with respect and learned what he was taught, he honored his parents.

It's not hard to see why the commandment speaks of honor rather than love. Love is a natural impulse born of our intense desire to be close to someone we need. The commandment simply assumes that children will love their parents. Love is a natural impulse; honor is a moral choice. These two drives push children in opposite directions, and in so doing create most of the tension and vitality in their relationships with parents. Honor separates them; love draws them together. Honor keeps a distance, maintains a certain reserve; love pull them close. Honor respects the gap between them; love bridges that gap. Honor is an act of the will that defers and stands back; love is an impulse of the heart that leans on a mother's breast at one stage and gently tucks a feeble mother to bed at another.

Honor and love need each other. Without love honor is frigid, strained, forced, infected with resentment, a hollow shell of polite anger. Without honor love lacks structure and is eventually destructive. Between parents and child, love without honor stands family life on its head, confuses the primal relationship of the human race. Honor is the moral fiber that holds the family together so that all the warm and loving, cold and hateful feelings between parent and child can be enjoyed and endured in a structure of loyalty and respect.

Why Should Children Honor Their Parents?

Let us first eliminate a few plausible but wrongheaded reasons for making honor a child's duty. First is the mystique of blood. What stands behind the duty of honor is not blood mystique but moral choice, not a sense of awe but a will for family order.

Second, the duty of honor is not a consequence of the sinfulness of the child. Children are no more sinful than parents are, and it is no more risky to let a child be free than it is to give a parent authority. Families would exist in a perfect world, and no doubt parents would be in charge even of perfect infants. The duty of honor, like most primary obligations, is rooted, not in a child's sinful nature, but in a divine design for human family. The parent has a whole realm of experience, wisdom and responsibility to be able to point out what is good in a given situation.

Third, we do not owe our parents honor out of gratitude for what they have done for us. Most of us probably do feel a great deal of gratitude to our parents, though many others store up bills of resentment for the grievous faults committed by parents. Where gratitude abounds, it is a powerful motive for obeying the command; but it cannot be the basic reason God uttered the command in the first place. The reason for the command must lie in the fabric of the family, in the role parents are called to play in the growth and nurture of children.

If there is a single reason why parents have a right to their children's respect, I suggest it is authority. Within the small society called family, in which joyful and painful human intimacies are experienced in the fundamental human relationship, one of the strong fibers that holds the alliance together is the authority of the parent.

Authority is not a popular facet of family life today, and countless homes have deliberately abandoned it, mistaking authority for a kind of tyranny which all who respect the rights of children should overthrow. Nevertheless, I am going to argue that parental authority, rightly understood, is the one quality all parents have which corresponds to the honor that children are asked to give them. Godly authority, moreover, is the backbone of family life. So important is it to the strength of the human community that the Lord God – in one of the five primal commandments for human life – called us all to honor our parents for their calling to nurture and guide us, the children set in their care.

Today – Authority in Crisis

People today have a fear of authority. Authority has become hopelessly confused with authoritarianism (people who rule out of an inadequacy in themselves and lack the courage to get any input from others being fearful of others who might displace them), though in truth they are utterly opposed to each other. Authoritarianism is sick compensation for weakness; authority is a healthy expression of strength. Authoritarian people stifle freedom; authority requires freedom to make it work. Authoritarianism works only when people surrender their own wills; authority works only when people give free and critical consent. Fear of authority is, in our time, actually a fear of authoritarianism, a confusion that cries for cure.

Contemporary fear of authoritarianism does not fully explain why parents have lost authority. Life itself has changed. The ongoing migration into cities crowds families into such close quarters that only a few can embrace anyone besides the parents and children. The movement of women out of the home into the office has drained the parental team of sheer energy to exercise authority. The psychologizing of life has heightened parents' awareness of their own emotional needs: what they often want in their passage years is a last chance to maximize their own experience and to "get with" their own feelings while they can still enjoy them. Their devotion to getting more out of life for themselves tends to drain them of the emotional energy they need daily to exert authority to guide their children.

While parents turn feverishly inward to their neglected psyches, their children's lives are complicated by revolutions in sexual styles, popular use of drugs, bombardment by the media with violence and sex, unrestricted mobility, and resignation of authority in the classroom. Being an authority with their children in this bewildering circus is almost too much for parents who want somehow to seize what is left of life for themselves. The temptation is to refer children to the experts outside of the family.

The Carnegie Council on the Family took a look at the crisis of the modern family and decided we should call it quits on the family as a human center for moral and spiritual nurture. Instead, we are told, we should settle for letting the family be a haven for emotional warmth. In other words, when we get home – all we want is to love one another and face no problems.

In a report written by Kenneth Kenniston, called *All Our Children*, the council suggests that the old-fashioned, self-sufficient family, in which parents could be relied upon to teach their children the important things of life, is a myth. In our complex world, parents are simply not competent [wrong conclusion] to prepare their children for taking a poised place in society. Kenniston goes on to say:

> "No longer able to do it all themselves, parents today are in some ways like the executives in a large firm – responsible for the smooth coordination of the many people and processes that must work together to produce the final product."

Parents shuffle children from authority to authority and from expert to expert (often in a very random way); their own chief business with the children is to provide emotional support. They have no authority of their own.

The one thing the Carnegie Report does not do is encourage parents themselves to recapture a moral sense of their own calling as authorities in their own families. Parents cannot give up authority without robbing their children – and eventually society – of strengths neither can do without. The first thing the child loses in a home without authority is a strong sense of his own identity. We become strong individuals when we spend our childhood in a strong family. The child with a clear sense of place in a family is likely to develop a clear sense of whom and what he is outside of it.

Secondly, it is only reasonable to suppose that loss of authority within the family will affect a child's ability to live with authority in society. Parents who give strong and purposeful leadership teach their children to live with and recognize true authority. If a child develops personally in an atmosphere where trust, loyalty, and honor are expected of him, he is well on his way toward a responsible life in society whose health depends on mutual trust, strong loyalties, and a critical caution with regard to all claims of authority. Permissive parents rob society of people who can distinguish genuine authority from its counterfeits.

Weak families produce uprooted individuals, unsure of their direction and therefore searching for some authority. We might add that they often find it in authoritarian substitutes all too ready, not only to lead, but to control.

Chapter 5

Parental Authority

Matthew 20:25-28 (NKJV) [25] But Jesus called them to *Himself* and said, *"You know that the rulers of the Gentiles lord it over them, and those who are great exercise authority over them.* [26] *Yet it shall not be so among you; but whoever desires to become great among you, let him be your servant.* [27] *And whoever desires to be first among you, let him be your slave—* [28] *just as the Son of Man did not come to be served, but to serve, and to give His life a ransom for many."*

Matthew 21:23-27 (NKJV) [23] Now when He came into the temple, the chief priests and the elders of the people confronted Him as He was teaching, and said, "By what authority are You doing these things? And who gave You this authority?" [24] But Jesus answered and said to them, *"I also will ask you one thing, which if you tell Me, I likewise will tell you by what authority I do these things:* [25] *The baptism of John—where was it from? From heaven or from men?"* And they reasoned among themselves, saying, "If we say, 'From heaven,' He will say to us, 'Why then did you not believe him?' [26] But if we say, 'From men,' we fear the multitude, for all count John as a prophet." [27] So they answered Jesus and said, "We do not know." And He said to them, *"Neither will I tell you by what authority I do these things.*

Matthew 28:18 (NKJV) [18] And Jesus came and spoke to them, saying, *"All authority has been given to Me in heaven and on earth.*

Proverbs 29:2 (NKJV) [2] When the righteous are in authority, the people rejoice; But when a wicked *man* rules, the people groan.

> **Titus 2:15** (NKJV) [15] Speak these things, exhort, and rebuke with all authority. Let no one despise you.

What is authority? Every time we are stopped in traffic by the police, every time we take an expert's word for it, every time we see a conductor move a great orchestra infallibly through a symphony, every time we submit our life to the promises and claims of the Word of God, we experience authority. What we experience is someone's assumption that he or she has the power and the right to lead us and tell us what to do or what to think.

Authority seems to be a blend of power and legitimacy, of might and right. It is a legitimate power to prevail over other people's wills. Sheer power without legitimacy is not real authority; the Nazis had power but not legitimacy in occupied France, and hence, no authority. But if you claim legitimacy without power, you cannot count on your authority.

What gives any person the right to use power of any kind over another person? From a biblical viewpoint, all authority comes from God, whether the institution of the family, church or civil government. The Creator ordains that human society be kept humanely ordered by vesting some offices with the right to control – to a limited extent – the behavior of certain people. But we must bring this belief about the ultimate source of authority into the dynamics of real life, for human authority works in human ways. We must ask how all human authority is mediated through human agencies and how we recognize authority when we see it.

There are three ways in which people get authority. The first is tradition. When people influence other people in the name of laws and customs which their society has believed in for all their history, they do so with authority. They gain authority as others feel their oneness with their own deepest reverence for the past which makes them what they are today. The second is legality. When people occupy positions of power according to the established rules of the group, they are given authority to govern people. The third is spiritual. When inspired persons call people to a new and better way of life, they are recognized as bearers of divine and righteous power to move people. In that sense they have spiritual authority.

A person, then, must be given authority, not seize it as one seizes power. At one level authority comes to someone before exercising power; and he or she expects people to recognize it. At another level, however, it is the people affected by authority who determine whether or not someone has it. People must believe and affirm that a person has authority; otherwise, in a very real way, they deprive him of power and, thereby, of effective authority.

We see, then, a dynamic dialogue between a person who claims authority – on the ground that he had been given the right – and those who believe him and by believing enable him to possess authority. A government, no matter how legitimate in point of law, loses authority when the people no longer believe it has the power or right to govern. A scientist's methods may be sound and her findings verified, but she does not have authority in her field until her peers credit her with it. Her intrinsic right is not enough; she needs to be believed in.

So, to be an authority we need investment. Not only from God or tradition or the legal system or our own experience, but also from the people over whom we seek to prevail, or whom we seek to lead, teach, or otherwise influence.

Jesus Illustrates the Dynamic of Personal Authority

Jesus had legitimate power to change people's souls, to redirect their lives, to lead them into a new world. No legal apparatus invested Him with authority; He wore no badge and never traveled in the company of a military escort. Yet he claimed supreme authority (Matt. 7:29; 28:18).

Yet while Jesus came with authority by virtue of Who He was, His legitimacy had to be believed. No one doubted that He had power. But some said His power was illegitimate – of the devil (Matt. 9:34) – and that He therefore had no authority, no right to lead people and influence their wills. Sometimes at least, He lost His power when people refused to believe the legitimacy of His claims. He could not do many miracles in Nazareth because the people did not believe that He had authority (Mark 6:5). In some way that we cannot quite grasp, He needed the faith of people in order to exercise authority.

What convinced people of Jesus' authority? People heard and saw and felt something in Jesus that made them believe He was a legitimate power. No doubt they sensed that He represented the spiritual tradition of messianic hope which was the essence of who they were as a people. But they conceded His right to prevail as a power in their lives also because they saw the very clear healing, helping, saving purpose in His power.

Jesus used power over them to heal, never to demand. He cured their diseases and asked nothing from them. He claimed to be Lord, yet He used His Lordship to liberate them. He claimed to be Master, yet He nurtured people into freedom. In short, His authority was the authority of a servant. In Paul's words, He emptied Himself of the unilateral authority He had simply by virtue of His divinity and became a servant (Phil. 2:1-5). Here was His secret. He was believable in His magnificent claim because He used power to serve people without enslaving them.

Richard Sennett concludes his splendid work on authority by saying:

> "To ask that power be nurturing and restrained is unreal – or that, at least, is the version of reality our history has inculcated in us." "Yet," he adds, "we must imagine that servant authority is real; we must keep the myth of a servant-authority alive as an ideal."

The gospel offers Jesus as that real ideal of the authority who uses power in order to serve (see John 13:14-17; Luke 22:24-27). His power nurtures us; and, nurtured, we credit Him with authority.

From Jesus we can draw a few tentative guidelines for thinking about the authority parents have to lead and teach and direct children. Authority is a union of legitimacy and power; the right to use power to influence people, even to prevail over them, gives a person what we call authority. A person's authority must be believed by the people he hopes to lead; no one can function as an authority unless people are willing to trust him. Persons have genuine authority only when they use power over people to nurture people into responsible freedom.

What we see, then, is that authority is a reality which exists only in a relationship where the authority-bearer and the authority-follower are active. People have no real authority unless they are trusted and believed; and no one deserves to be trusted unless he or she helps people be free.

Parental Authority – Derived from the Family

Why does an adult who happens to conceive and channel a human being into the world have the right to shape and form that child's life? It is because the mother and father are smarter and wiser than a child? Hardly, since other adults are smarter and wiser than the parent and they could teach the child even more efficiently? Is it because the child owes parents obedience in return for the lavish sum they spend on his or her care? Hardly, the right to expect a return on your investment does not give you authority to influence another person at the core of his life. No, if parents have authority, it comes from their special roles within the troubled community of care we call a family.

So we should ask what a family is. A family is a group of people bound together in a covenant of care for one another. Though blood is a family's natural bond, it does not create a family. The sheer fact that people live together under one roof does not create a family, contrary to the U. S. Census Bureau's definition of a family as "two or more persons related by blood, adoption, or marriage and residing together." In a moral sense, what binds people together as a family is the covenant of loyalty to one another from birth to death.

When two people bring a child into the world, they are called to be its caretakers. This calling, though parents may never give it thought, is the first ingredient of a family. Parents are invested with the calling by virtue of accepting the child as their own, and they turn their little circle into a family when they covenant in their hearts to fulfill that calling.

The child, in turn, gradually learns to trust the parents to be his caregivers. This trust adds the second ingredient to a family. The child begins to trust that the adults hovering over him will be there to feed him, to let him touch human flesh, to give warmth against the cold, and above all to keep from falling into the terrible dangers a small child fears. The trust grows as the parents begin to give more than physical and emotional security. Gradually they tell the child what they believe to be true and right about life and its meaning. Again, the child trusts the parent to take care of him.

But why should there be families at all? Why should societies be made up of these countless clusters of loyalty-bound communities? Conventional liberal wisdom has it that families are here to provide emotional support in a world that does not much care about us. The family is a "haven in a heartless world," a refuge from a society in which everybody is out to beat us to the glimmering prizes. In the family, we have a place where we can be coddled, cuddled, and comforted in intimacy. In a way, families are therapy centers for harried spirits.

The Judeo-Christian perspective, however, sees the circle of covenanted care as the right setting for the nurture of children into commitment to what is right and true about life. Parents are parents mainly to take care of the child's initiation into faith and morals. And the two go together. Morality has to do with what is truly important and right about life, and what is important about life depends on what is true about God. So, the heart of family is the parent's calling to pass on the moral and spiritual reality of life to their children. The covenant of caretaking, then, creates the family. In this context alone we can understand how a parent has authority and why the child has an obligation to honor the parent.

A parent is not a spillover from our romantic passions, nor a product of society's requirement that parents provide their offspring with bed and board, nor a little circle of people deriving emotional support from living together. Nor a social contrivance from keeping our broods in control, one which could become obsolete if a social planner were to find a better one. In a Judeo-Christian sense, family is rooted in the Creator's design for the ongoing nurture of children who bring faith and moral value into the next generation. To undermine, neglect, or replace it is to wreck the core community that makes all other community possible.

Parental Authority – Focused on Faith and Morality

Unique to a person's authority as a parent is being a teacher of what is right and true about life. Naturally, a parent has other sorts of authority too. A mother may require her children to do chores, for example, but her clout in the kitchen is not basically different from a mess sergeant's clout in the mess hall. A mother acts in her special role as mother when she is, in the thousand ways available to her, helping her children know what is worth living for and what is worth dying for.

The mother may be wrong, of course. She may use her authority to teach her children unorthodox notions about God and misinformed ideas of morality. But she does not lose her authority if she lacks orthodoxy or profundity; parental authority is rooted in a calling to teach one's children what one believes to be true and right, not in expertise.

Better that a child grow up with some mistaken notions about what matters much than to grow up with the notion that nothing much matters. Because, who is an expert on God and morality? As Stanley Hauerwas points out, "In matters moral there are no experts; and therefore all parents are charged with forming their children's lives according to what they know best."

What I have been claiming for parental authority calls into question a modern liberal premise about family life. Conventional wisdom tells us that we should respect children's sovereign rights to make up their minds about matters religious and moral. In the liberal credo, everyone in the family is an individual with equal authority on these matters. Since nobody is an expert on belief, a father has no right to foist his beliefs on his children. Authority has to rest on proven expertise; if a mother lacks it, she should defer to an expert who has it. Only an authoritarian parent would send children into the world with a bias about morals and a prejudice toward faith. The role of parents is to keep their children in a moral and religious vacuum until they are ready to decide for themselves. The only really important thing a parent may teach about these matters is that they are not important enough for a parent fervently to care that the child continue in the faith and morality of the family.

From the perspective of biblical morality, liberalism's family philosophy is a disaster. For the one reason the Bible gives for seeing the family as the basic component of the human community is that the family is the appropriate setting for a child to learn the core values of life and the meaning and purpose of existence.

There is a curious twist to the working of authority in a family. True authority, I have tried to say, is exercised – and in a way created – in dialogue. You cannot exercise authority unless the people you want to influence believe in you. This is as true of parental authority as of any other. A parent needs to exercise authority in order to awaken the child's belief in it. Belief for a child takes the form of trust. Where the simplest, least educated, and skilled parent believes in his own authority as a parent the child learns to trust him. The courage to tell my son or my daughter what I believe helps make me credible in their eyes. A child does not lose trust when a mother makes a mistake, or when a father exposes his ignorance on a point of theology or ethics. A child loses trust when he senses that his father and or mother does not really believe what they say they believe.

Parental Authority – Aimed at the Child's Freedom

The goal of parental authority is freedom. The parents' authority aims at releasing the child from their authority. This does not mean that parents lead their children toward freedom from authority, but that they use parental authority to help the child develop a responsible freedom that will enable him to live with – and be critical of – all other human authority.

The authority pattern of the family teaches a child how to live freely and critically within the authority structures of society. Living with parents who believe in their own authority and understand its purpose, children learn what authority is really for. Thus they learn how to size up anyone who claims to be an authority. Any society has powerful people who claim the right to influence and control others. Cultists, on the fringes of society, religious and secular people alike, deploy mesmerizing gifts to seduce people who never have had a life experience with genuinely caring authority into giving up their freedom for the sake of security.

Every parent who claims the right to respect for his authority must keep this in mind; parental authority aims at critical freedom under all authority.

Parental Authority – Limited by the Child's Rights

We cannot discuss parent's authority without also talking about children's rights. The contemporary concern for the rights of children is not just faddish sentimentality. When the prophets summoned Israel to seek justice for the orphans and other weaker citizens, they were speaking for children's rights. And when Jesus added His terrible indictment against anyone who caused a child to sin, He declared the divine right of all children to be free from adult abuse (Matt. 18:6).

Children's rights no more undermine parental authority than the civil rights of an individual cancel out the authority of government. In both cases, rights only limit authority and keep it in bounds. But the rights of children are limited as well. For this reason we must speak as concretely as possible about them.

A list of children's rights within the family should probably include the following:

- **The right to life.** Every person's right to life is a moral armor for the child against a selfish decision by parents to let handicapped babies die or even cause their deaths.

- **The right to care.** No child chooses to be born. Brought helpless into existence by two adults, he has a claim on them for responsible care during the time of his dependence on them.

- **The right to safety from abuse.** No parent can guarantee a child safety from all the ills to which the flesh is heir. But parents can covenant to keep their own hands from abusing the children in their care. No parent can ever justify battering a son or daughter – with hands or mouth – on the ground of having authority over his own children.

- **The right to fairness.** In a family of more than one child, each one has a right to fairness. Parents must distribute their gifts to all children fairly. A child may not have a right to birthday presents, for example, but if one child gets them, the other children have a right to the same sort of favors. The right to emotional fairness is just as important; the ugly duckling had a right to as much as the beautiful swan. No child can reasonably expect perfect fairness from any mortal parents, but every child has the right at least to a parent's intention to be fair.

- **The right to unconditional acceptance.** A child has a right to be affirmed, accepted, and loved unconditionally by the parents who decided the child should exist. No parent has the authority to say or imply that a child is too evil or ugly or dull or lazy to accept. Parental authority never gives anyone a right to reject his child.

Thus far we have been speaking of children's moral rights within the family. It may be, however, if parents are guilty of gross violations, that the state's coercive authority may have to invade the normally sovereign sphere of the family to protect the legal rights of the child. Parents obviously do not have absolute authority over their children. But we must face the consequences for the family if we grant the state carte blanche to override parental authority.

Do we have evidence for thinking that judges, lawyers, bureaucrats, and social workers are likely in the long run to be more reliable protectors of children's welfare than fallible parents? And even if parents egregiously violate their children's rights at times, what would happen if society at large, if this foundational min-society, the family, were completely to forfeit its sovereignty to the state?

Was it necessary to dig so deeply into the notion of parental authority to get a grip on the child's duty to honor his or her parents? I think so. Honor is an unsentimental thing brushing close to the heart of morality, a little moral finger pointing to the structure of creation's most delicate order, the family. For a child to learn to honor his or her parents is to learn to respect the human incarnation or moral authority. Parents have a calling, not just to feed their offspring or to protect them from the hardships of a human jungle, but to share with them their deepest beliefs about God and His will for the human family.

The only quality parents share which entitles them at all to children's honor is a calling to teach their children what is true and what is right about God and His world. They have a right to teach, to influence, to guide, and to persuade their children about what they, the parents, believe about the core matters of life. Their embodiment of this right makes them worthy of respect. If they forfeit their calling, by default, fear, or laziness, their loss of honor is their own fault.

Chapter 6

The Family in Community Life

So far we have focused on building a framework for family life. Particularly, we have seen that passing on the faith to our children is a primary function of the home. In this chapter, we will focus on the need for the family to be part of a local church family. This is essential if we are going to have the additional divine reinforcement needed to complete the job of seeing our children fully embrace the elementary principles of the faith for their own lives.

God never intended children to be trained by parents who were outside the context of a local church community. No such model exists in the Old Testament amongst Jewish families or in the New Testament in Christian families. The directives to believing families were always given in the context of a family of families. This is even more important in a technological culture where extended families are strewn all over the country and immediate families are fragmented under the strain of individualism. We will again turn our attention to a community household text, Titus 2:1-9.

> **Titus 2:1-9** (NKJV) [1] But as for you, speak the things which are proper for sound doctrine: [2] that the older men be sober, reverent, temperate, sound in faith, in love, in patience; [3] the older women likewise, that they be reverent in behavior, not slanderers, not given to much wine, teachers of good things— [4] that they admonish the young women to love their husbands, to love their children, [5] to be discreet, chaste, homemakers, good, obedient to their own husbands, that the word of God may not be blasphemed. [6] Likewise, exhort the young men to be sober-minded, [7] in all things showing yourself *to be* a pattern of good

works; in doctrine *showing* integrity, reverence, incorruptibility, [8] sound speech that cannot be condemned, that one who is an opponent may be ashamed, having nothing evil to say of you. [9] Exhort bondservants to be obedient to their own masters, to be well pleasing in all *things,* not answering back,

As you ponder the above text it is important to consider the following questions:

- What is the role of older members in the church community to the younger?

- Does the admonition for older women to be teaching younger women imply that older men should be teaching aspects of family life to the younger men?

- What kinds of things should the older men and women be teaching the younger?

- In this passage, how is the local church community helping younger parents carry out their responsibilities?

Titus 2 is a beautiful summary of everything contained in the Pastoral Epistles. Sound doctrine & proper ordering of life in the church has little, if any, significance unless it produces changed lives that demonstrate a high quality of life and love. Older men and women are to be leaders and examples to the younger. The assumption is that they have lived long enough to sift and sort out the differences between that which is truly abiding in value and that which is of little or no value. Aging can be a rich and rewarding experience rather than a threatening and frightening process. Paul instructs us in the rich potential of the aging process.

Four goals are set forth for men. And the word "likewise" in verse 3 implies that these same goals are just as valid for women.

1. **Sobriety** – clear headedness. Picture a person who has achieved perspective in life – or who is not under the influence of outside forces (alcohol, money, anger, lust or greed). Whatever the aging experiences should do for us, they should enable us to develop a perspective in which our values are brought into line with God's intentions for us. The hardest thing for us older folks to accept is that the younger generation is going to learn some of the things we have learned by trial and error. We should be concerned however, if the same people are chasing the same goals that they started pursuing 30 years ago. Our perspectives and values grow in sobriety as we age, a clear-headed way of viewing everything around us.

2. **Reverence** – serious and mature behavior. This does not mean dullness. Reverence for life, for people, for nature – everyone and everything around you.

3. **Temperate** – prudent or sensible. It portrays a person whose actions have a high degree of correspondence with his best judgment. Paul as a younger man describes his struggle (Rom. 7:19). Maturing is narrowing the gap between our best judgment and our actual behavior. It involves mind and feelings to shape our judgment and our judgments. When judgment is simply rational it is cold and impersonal. When judgment is simply feelings it can be irresponsible.

4. **Product of first three***: "Sound in faith, in love, and in patience."* Faith has a way of growing with the years, not necessarily in the intellectual sense, but in the sense of simply trusting God more. As I grow older I may develop more intellectual questions and struggle the more that I study and learn, but also find myself trusting in God more and more. Growth in love is growth in our ability to act in the best interest of others and this ties us back to

patience and endurance that enables us not merely to survive but to transform hardships into things of beauty for God.

Yet another goal of maturing is set forth specifically to the older women, "that they be reverent in behavior." The language describes a sacred priest carrying out her duties. The picture is one of a person who sees her entire life as worship to God (Rom, 12:1). The word "service" is the word used of for priestly ministry in the temple. Maturing in Christ is to grow in the awareness that all of life is sacred and that everything we do has a direct relationship to God. Happy is the person who sees desk and kitchen sinks as altars rather than artifacts.

It is clear that maturing can be the best part of the aging process. We cannot mature without aging. The tragedy is aging without maturity.

We find ourselves in a household text that deals with the household of faith – a local community. Titus was a letter written to Titus by Paul, instructing him in how to fully establish the new churches on the island of Crete in the first principles of the faith. He was to appoint a solid team of elders in every church. One of the reasons was that the church needed to be protected from false teachers who would come in with philosophies that would upset whole families. Therefore, strengthening and establishing families in these churches was clearly part of Paul's original intention when he wrote the letter.

In this passage, Paul addressed the conduct of older men, women, younger men, older women, and younger women. Older women were to teach the younger women. The structure of the passage is to list the lifestyle that is to accompany a committed disciple according to his station in life. Teachers like Titus were to exhort each local church family member to learn his or her "lifestyle" (2:15). An example of the way each family member learns is the older women teaching the younger women. By implication of the example, older men should be teaching younger men. Part of the sphere of this teaching is our character. Part of it centers around our family lives. It is clear, then, that the local church community is to play a major role in reinforcing families. It must help them live according to the household guidelines set out in the New Testament, a major goal of which is passing on the faith to the children.

Today, we have little sense of these reinforcements in our churches. We have few community-wide traditions, rites of passage or bar mitzvahs, and catechisms or didaches. The further any culture progresses into a technological society, the more it fragments the extended family and eventually community life. God's design is for every family in every culture to be part of a local church family. Ideally there is the immediate family, which is reinforced by its own extended family of believing families – parents, grandparents, aunts and uncles, etc., several generations deep - and finally, they are all part of a local church community – an extended family of families. We know little of this in our churches today. No wonder young parents feel lost. And it's no wonder that we are losing 60-70% of our children from the faith, as we enter the early stages of a post-Christian era and postmodern culture.

No one addresses the issue of the fragmentation of the family in a technological society better that Stephen Clark in *Man and Woman in Christ*. Here he elaborates on the absolute necessity for families and churches in a technological society to understand these matters.

> "In traditional society, the family consists of more than the nuclear unit of husband, wife, and offspring. The traditional family consists of a sizable group of people and includes many conjugal units linked through some structure based on common descent. This wide set of committed kinship relationships exists regardless of whether the group lives together in one building. The larger family, kinship group, or clan has several important functions. It provides financial aid to the individual conjugal unit in times of special need, and often functions as a unit of economic operation. For example, a family farm or business

often belongs to the larger kinship group instead of the head of a conjugal family. The kinship grouping therefore serves as the social security, welfare, and insurance system. The members of the larger family also share one another's good fortune. If one member arrives at a position of power or wealth, the entire kinship grouping can expect to benefit. Side by side with this strong kinship system is a committed village, neighborhood, occupational, or class grouping. These groupings sometimes perform functions and fulfill roles similar to those of the kinship grouping. The conjugal unit thus finds its place in the wider set of relationships and commitments provided by the kinship system and the neighborhood-type grouping..."

"In technological society, most of the functions once associated with family life are transferred to the realm of mass institutions. Economic life occurs within distinct economic institutions (businesses, factories, offices) separated from people's homes. Hospitals, clinics, doctors, and nurses care for the sick, and most people are born and die in a medical institution apart from the family. Infirmed aged are cared for in hospitals, convalescent homes, and retirement centers. Financial support is provided by insurance agencies, loan agencies, social security systems and welfare departments. Most education (except for the earliest stages) occurs at a school or on the job. Religious education is provided by Sunday school or catechism class. Police and standing armies assume all defense functions. Even leisure becomes less the province of the family, and more the province of peer groups and "friends."...

"The Christian community should provide a supportive environment for family life. The forces of technological society have weakened the kinship network that traditionally provided a valuable supportive environment for the family. In technological society, the Christian community should assume those supportive functions once performed by the kinship network. The community should be like an extended family. It should not compete with the family for the loyalty of the individual (as sometimes happens in socialist societies). Nor should it operate according to principles completely different from those obtaining in the family (as is the case of most technological societies). Instead, the Christian community should be a larger fabric of personal relationships into which the family unit is tightly integrated. Existing extended family relationships which are still cohesive need not be weakened, but can be fit into the broader community support system. In fact, a Christian community can often help restore healthy kinship structures."

A Christian community can provide support for the family unit in many ways, most of which were once provided by the kinship network. The community provides the larger social environment which supports family relationships and family order by maintaining a consistent and uniform pattern of social roles. Like the members of an extended family, the brothers and sisters in the larger Christian community should also provide supportive relationships among the men (husbands) and among the women (wives) in the community. These relationships should strengthen the men and women in their distinctive responsibilities and also prevent the women from being isolated in their nuclear family units. In general, the community should provide women with ways to be fully a part of communal life.

Many modern people, Christians and non-Christians alike, have attempted to strengthen the family by directly buttressing the nuclear family unit. In many ways this seems to be the most obvious course of action. However, the evidence from anthropology and social history indicates that the nuclear family is only strong when it exists in the context of a larger extended-family system. Such a system need not be completely built on lineage, but it must involve the commitment of the nuclear family to a larger social grouping.

In the technological societies of the West, we tend to see the family as an isolated unit, self-sustaining, and in many ways a spring-board for the individual to pursue his or her own life goals and career. Rarely do we view the family as a subset of a larger unit – the local church family. Therefore, we do not think of the local church family as responsible to share in the process of reinforcing, in indispensable ways, the passing on of the faith to children. We need to explore the significance of the larger church family in reinforcing parents in the process of passing on the faith to their children.

Consider the following questions as a way to strengthen involvement in community life:

- In what ways is a family that is isolated at a significant disadvantage from a family that is a vital part of a local church community?

- In what ways might a true community with mature older men and women strengthen the parents in their role of passing on the faith to their children?

- What problems are likely to surface in an inexperienced young family that is isolated from a local church community? In a harried two-career family?

- How might a church structure its programs and community life if it really saw itself as an extended family with part of its task being to reinforce parents in passing on the faith to their children?

It is my hope that you will grow in conviction as to the importance that a true community has in building a generation of children who fully embrace the faith. You can affirm this conviction by your commitment to completely involve your family in the life of a community of believers. If you are a young parent, think through which older women or men you could look to for wisdom. If you are an older man or women, think through the families in the church with whom you could invest time. If you are a grandparent or great-parent, think through how to help reinforce passing on the faith to your grandchildren. If a single adult, make yourself available to serve families in your church family at a deep enough level to become like an extended family member. If you are a young single person planning on marriage, build your life and your initial life plan deeply into the life of a local church community, and learn to live as a vital part of true community life, purposing to set an example for the soon-to-be young adults to follow.

Chapter 7
Managing Our Households

Up to now we have looked at how to build a framework for passing on the faith to our children. We have seen the importance of God's overall design – the lines of authority clearly established for children, parents who are committed to training their children in the faith, and a local church family committed to reinforcing the parents in the whole process. Yet it still has to be accomplished. How is it all going to come together? In this chapter we will work on this very problem – how to manage the entire process. It is possible to know the entire framework of God's design and yet fail to manage the process. After all, each child is at least an 18-year project and more if you count the final transition years. That means that each child is a very big project. How do we ensure that the process is working, well integrated, and turning out children from each family who fully embrace the faith? The passage that gives us the key to pulling it all together is 1 Timothy 3:4-5.

> **1 Timothy 3:4-5** (NKJV) [4] one who rules his own house well, having *his* children in submission with all reverence [5] (for if a man does not know how to rule his own house, how will he take care of the church of God?);

As you think about this passage you must think through some questions:

- Who is responsible to manage the entire process, seeing that the children are under authority and that the faith is properly transmitted?

- Is a man actually responsible for the outcome of the life choices of his children (Titus 1:5-6)?

- What does this tell us about the importance of the role of the father?

- In this context, what exactly does it mean to "manage his own household well"? What is included in that responsibility?

Reflecting on the passage we see that it is part of the extended community household text, beginning at 1 Timothy 2 and continuing through chapter 6. In this particular context, Paul listed qualifications for being an elder in a local community. The reasoning goes like this: If a man cannot manage the affairs of his own household well, how can he be entrusted, along with a team of other men, to manage the affairs of the household of God-the local church community. Therefore, even though the passage is within a list of qualifications for elders, it clearly is a pattern for all men since elders are made up of men who show exceptional character and leadership skill in their own houses.

What exactly is a man - in this case a father – responsible for? Managing his own household. The term *manage* is used twice. What does it mean? There are three clues into the precise meaning in these two verses alone. First is the actual meaning of the Greek word for *manage*. It literally means "to preside over, to stand before, to rule or lead." The second clue is in the term used for taking care of the church of God. That term literally means "to diligently care for, to take great thought to your care of others." The third clue is the explanation of a key central task in the managing of his household – the management of his children. This means that a key task of managing his household is bringing his children up in the discipline and instruction of the Lord. At the very heart of his responsibility to manage his household is managing the entire project of the lives of his children, including passing on the faith to them. If he is not able to manage them, leading them to the faith, then he is not doing his job well.

A parallel passage is Titus 1:5-6. Here he sheds additional light on this household management that is expected of the father. This passage focuses again on an elder's household. This time the expectation is that one who is qualified to lead the household of God must have children who are believers and who are not rebellious. Some say that this just refers to children who are faithful. But in this context, rebellion would clearly include a rejection of the faith, for that is the heart of the entire management process. If we expect the results we want – children who continue solidly in the faith – then the father must lead, carefully manage, and oversee the process.

Another insightful passage is 1 Timothy 5:14, where Paul encouraged young widows to get married again. He told them that a central sphere of their focus was to have children and to "keep house." That is not the best translation. The word *oikosdespoteo*, which literally means "house" (*oikos*) and "despot" (*despoteo*). The wife is to be the despot of the house. The image here is not a cold, cruel dictator, for in all the passages where mothers are mentioned in the New Testament, they are characterized as kind and nurturing to their children. The point is that they are to care for and watch over every detail of the home management plan like a despot, guarding and carrying out every aspect of it. It is impossible for a man to manage his household with the kind of care described in these passages without a wife who is fully devoted to the plan. In our life, both of our children are adults and very productive, committed believers within our local church family. This would not have been possible without my wife Bernice's enormous commitment to our overall plan for passing on the faith to our children.

The point is simply this: the key to pulling it all together – the establishing of discipline and authority in the home, the training of the children, the integrating of the teaching and reinforcement of the local church family – is the diligent management of the entire process by the father. It will never happen the way God intended it unless the father assumes his God-given responsibility and unless he pursues that responsibility with passion and careful attention to every facet of the process. Since each child is at least an 18-year project, this is probably the most monumental of all tasks for a father – even over his lifework!

So what is involved in this household management process? From our work in this book, we can pull together several core elements to begin carrying it out. It obviously includes an enormous amount of work on the part of both parents.

George W. Knight III, a New Testament professor and significant contributor to the *Council for Biblical Manhood and Womanhood*, wrote the following:

> "The care and management of the home is another area in which Christians need to implement Biblical principles carefully. The Scriptures present the direct management of the children and the household as the realm of responsibility of the wife and mother. First Timothy 5:14 says that wives are "to manage their homes" (NIV). The Greek word *oikodespote*, which is rendered 'manage,' is a very forceful term. Proverbs 31 indicates some of the many ways in which this management is carried out (cf., e.g., verses 26 and 27: 'She opens her mouth in wisdom, and the teaching of kindness is on her tongue. She looks well to the ways of her household, and does not eat the bread of idleness,' NASB). The husband must recognize this calling and grant her the necessary and appropriate freedom of operation under his leadership. At the same time, the wife must recognize that her management is to be conducted in submission to her husband's leadership, who is responsible for the overall management of the household (cf. Titus 2:5, 'to be busy at home ... and to be subject to their husbands'). The Apostle Paul says that the man is responsible to manage his own household well (1 Timothy 3:4-5).

"Although the wife and mother will have the most contact with the children, especially when they are young, and therefore will have the most direct responsibility for supervising them, the husband and father is held responsible for instruction and oversight of the children (Eph. 6:4; 1 Tim. 3:4). It is imperative that fathers and mothers carry out this joint task in such a way that the leadership of both over the children is maintained and the headship of both over the children is maintained and the headship of the father over the family is manifest. Thus neither should allow the children to play one parent off against the other in seeking to contravene the other's commands or prohibitions. The parents should resolve those questions in private away from the children; in public they should uphold each other's decisions, especially the mother upholding the headship of the father. Fathers should exercise an appropriate leadership by being careful to avoid exasperating or provoking comments or commands (Eph. 6:4; Col. 3:21) that not only discourage or anger their children but also provide occasion for their wives to feel the necessity of intervening and make it more difficult for them to be subject to their husbands' leadership. Exasperating or provoking comments or commands include commands that are unjust and comments that are given in a callous or unfeeling way. All parental give-and-take before children should manifest mutual respect and communicate before the children that the husband genuinely loves and respects his wife and the wife, too respects and desires to submit to the leadership of her husband and their father. Such an attitude can itself be the best setting for the children to learn their own necessary submission to both father and mother."

It is not enough to just understand God's design for family life, especially as it pertains to the central task of passing on the faith to our children. We must think through how to put it into operation. This calls for a very significant "management" process, which necessarily falls on the father. So many of the books today are nothing more than shallow how-to-books with simple remedies for solving the problems of the family and reversing the exodus of our children from the faith.

Consider the following questions. They have been designed to help you think through the directive of being serious, diligent managers of our households.

- What is likely to happen to a household with no clear leadership? With no clear, careful management?

- Why is it important for the father to be deeply involved in managing the household? Can he not just give general oversight?

- In light of what has been studied in the household texts in this book, what are the main elements of family life which need to be managed?

- What would be the signs of a well-managed household? The outcomes?

In light of this study think about what is involved in a father carefully managing his household? You may want to list any changes that need to be made in your current household management. Men, it's time to reaffirm your commitments to assume full responsibility for leading your households. Women, you can also reaffirm your commitments to follow your husbands' leadership. As husbands and wives, make a commitment to building a master plan for passing on the faith to your children.

If you are a divorced or a single parent, you will need to carefully think through the management of the faith development of your children because it will be more difficult. Build a master plan to make the best use of your time and opportunities with your children, and incorporate others in your extended family and church family.

If you are not married, you can still begin work on a master plan for managing a household, and gain as many skills as you can now.

If older or widowed, think through how to manage your own household in such a way as to make the largest possible ongoing contribution to the continued faith development of your children or grandchildren or others' children.

Chapter 8
Parental Obedience to God's Commands

> **Deuteronomy 5:29** (NKJV) ²⁹ Oh, that they had such a heart in them that they would fear Me and always keep all My commandments, that it might be well with them and with their children forever!
>
> **2 Corinthians 12:14** (NKJV) ¹⁴ Now *for* the third time I am ready to come to you. And I will not be burdensome to you; for I do not seek yours, but you. For the children ought not to lay up for the parents, but the parents for the children.

In order to fulfill all that God has promised, there must be a heart of obedience in a generation of parents. It takes sacrifice, dedication, and selflessness for a generation of parents to take the time to make an investment in their children. It takes more than vision. Many can be inspired by vision, and this is needed, but the purpose of the inspiration is to cause us to obey. It is part of our sinful nature to neglect obedience when we do not see the immediate results that we feel are justified by our actions. However, without obedience, all that God promises will be but a dream.

Nothing substitutes for obedience. Mere sacrifice, token appreciation, and even monetary investments are no substitute for obedience to God's Word. We need to see beyond our own lives and beyond the lives of our children if we really wish to fulfill God's will in the earth within our generation. Then, we need to be willing to simply obey God and trust Him with the results. Let us ponder the commands of Scripture regarding the education of our children, and put our hands to the plow, raising consecutive generations to receive God's Kingdom!

Cultivating Obedience as our Primary Response

> **Deuteronomy 6:4-9** "Hear, O Israel: The Lord our God, the Lord is one! [5] You shall love the Lord your God with all your heart, with all your soul, and with all your strength. [6] "And these words which I command you today shall be in your heart. [7] You shall teach them diligently to your children, and shall talk of them when you sit in your house, when you walk by the way, when you lie down, and when you rise up. [8] You shall bind them as a sign on your hand, and they shall be as frontlets between your eyes. [9] You shall write them on the doorposts of your house and on your gates.

We are commanded to love God and teach our children. This teaching is systematic (morning, noon, and night), and is to be a permanent part of every area of our lives (our hands, or our labor; between our eyes, or what we see as our children's potential; on our posts, or our lives outside our homes and our business activities.) This portion of Scripture is considered a pivotal verse in the Old Testament Law and is part of the Jewish Mezuzah put on the doorpost of the home. We must begin to educate our children in God's ways because we love to obey Him.

> **Psalm 78:5** For He established a testimony in Jacob, And appointed a law in Israel, Which He commanded our fathers, That they should make them known to their children;

The theme of obedience in relation to training children is at the heart of the Old Testament Law, family life, and responsibility. The verse above is considered a pivotal Psalm, once again emphasizing the training of children. Throughout the Old Testament, as well as the New, we are commanded to train our children in the ways of the Lord.

Choosing to Obey the Lord

At its root, it is a matter of choosing obedience. Just how important is this response of obedience?

> **Deuteronomy 11:26-29** "Behold, I set before you today a blessing and a curse: [27] the blessing, if you obey the commandments of the Lord your God which I command you today; [28] and the curse, if you do not obey the commandments of the Lord your God, but turn aside from the way which I command you today, to go after other gods which you have not known. [29] Now it shall be, when the Lord your God has brought you into the land which you go to possess, that you shall put the blessing on Mount Gerizim and the curse on Mount Ebal.
>
> **Proverbs 1:7** The fear of the Lord is the beginning of knowledge, But fools despise wisdom and instruction.
>
> **John 14:15** "If you love Me, keep My commandments.

Obedience is the beginning, not the end, of serving God. We don't gradually slide into obedience, we must begin to obey what we know is God's command! We choose to obey what we know is right. We choose to make it our life's desire. God places the desire within us, by His grace, but we must choose to lay hold upon what God had placed there. Our knowledge of his commandments may grow with time, but we must choose to obey each commandment of His Word as we learn of our responsibility to Him.

Obedience is a natural result of the fear of the Lord. God only knows how much grief, pain, and suffering we endure in this life as a direct result of our reaping a curse upon our lives due to our choosing to disobey the clear commands of the Word of God.

God gives us the ability to obey through His grace as a result of Jesus' death on the cross and subsequent resurrection, but we still must choose to obey in order to have His ability appropriated in us.

Gaining a Conviction for Christian Education

Using the definition from Noah Webster's 1828 Dictionary, we can state that Christ is to be Lord of "all that series of instruction and discipline which is intended to enlighten the understanding, correct the temper, and form the manners and habits of youth, and fit them for usefulness in their future stations."

This definition, along with the instruction of Deuteronomy 6:7 to teach children at all times periodically throughout each day, would seem to indicate that *Christian education is a life training, and includes far more than school.*

It would be proper to say that the Christian school movement is a restoration of one aspect of Christian education, that being the formal discipline of the mind as an extension of the responsibility given to parents. Educational training is always taking place, however. The key question is whether or not consistent education that is distinctly Christian is taking place. If it is not, our children grow up living in two worlds, one that is Christian, and another that is not Christian. This double-minded training will produce unstable Christians at best, (James 1:8). The conviction that needs to be gained is one that will settle for nothing less than consistent training in all avenues under one's control, so that our children can grow up and face a crooked and perverse generation, shining as lights (Philippians 2:15-16).

Providentially, God began to wake up believers in America to their primary duty of obedience through the increasingly pagan courts of our land. In the early 1970's, a case was tried that would set the direction for almost two decades in the way in which believers were to be viewed in relation to the protection of their beliefs.

The Yoder decision involving an Amish individual who felt it was sin to send his children to a government school was rendered in 1972. Although the fact that the case was held is an indictment upon the secular reasoning and improper role of civil government in education, it nonetheless helped believers to clarify obedience from convenience, or what the courts called conviction and preference. The most eloquent exponent of the truths of this case was David Gibbs, an attorney from the Christian Law Association.

As we share the meaning of conviction from the court's point of view, remember that we do this only to illustrate the necessity of obedience to God. We do not gain "conviction" for the purpose of protecting our beliefs, but as our primary response to God and His Word. When we deal with conviction, and what it really is in relation to Christian education, we must also consider what the courts have called preference.

In contrasting these two kinds of "belief", one can better understand what it means to be obedient to God's commands, and what we may have to sacrifice in order to obey His Word.

Simply stated, a conviction is a belief that you hold so strongly and are so convinced that the Word of God teaches, having had it confirmed by the Holy Spirit to your heart, that you will not change it, no matter what the cost! For a Christian, every command of Scripture regarding our lifestyle and conduct before God and man, should be an eventual conviction. Obviously, however, we are all at varying degrees of growth, and therefore the number and quality of our convictions will grow and increase as we walk with the Lord and understand more of what He requires of us through His Word. A conviction is no "impulse", or "goose bump". It is something we know is required of us by God and has been firmly planted within our hearts by the Holy Spirit through His Word!

A preference, on the other hand, is a strongly held belief, just as a conviction, yet one will change it when enough pressure or inconvenience comes our way. This belief will waver and change with the circumstances, rather than remaining absolute. To better explain the difference between a preference and a conviction, let me quote from an article in The Capsule, a Christian digest of information on education.

David Gibbs of the Christian Law Association is summarized in an article on the topic of conviction and preference:

> "The courts recognize a preference as a strong belief. Such a belief may motivate one to full time service in the name of his faith. It may cause another to be an energetic 'soul winner'. While still others may give large sums of money in loyalty to the belief they hold. But – as long as those persons reserve the right to some day, some time, change their action it is classified as a preference and not a conviction. If they truly believe that God demands a certain standard, certain action, and they dare not change in the face of adverse circumstances – then that becomes a conviction. Most Christians try to go on a percentage basis with the commandments in God's Word, but obedience to Scripture is never an option. Either we obey the Word or we abandon it. There are five circumstances, which the courts note will cause a man to change his stand if his belief is a preference rather than a conviction. These include the pressure of your friends; your family; a law suit; going to jail; and the fear of death."

The article goes on to quote David Gibbs as saying:

> "... for a Christian parent to give his child a non-Christian education is a lie."

One must realize, however, that on the other side of the coin, simply sending your child to a Christian school or home-schooling your child in no way evidences automatically that you as a parent have a convictional relationship of obedience with God or His Word in the area of education. The real question is, what are you doing and teaching in your home that makes the total life experience of your child Christian? If you are not really practicing Christianity at home, then questions such as these could sway your involvement in Christian education:

- What if the school was farther away, more expensive, or more inconvenient in some way, would you change your conviction?

- Will you be willing to teach your children at home through employing tutors if you are not capable and there is no other option to give your child what he needs academically?

- Would you trust that what God commands He will faithfully provide the means to fully obey? (see 1st Thessalonians 5:24; Philippians 4:13, 19).

We need to be honest and ask why we do some of the things that we do. The Christian school movement in the 1970's and early 1980's grew at a tremendous rate, and now the home school movement is taking center stage at the fastest growing movement in America and possibly around the world. The real question is, are Christian schools and home schools growing and starting for the right reasons? Are we primarily beginning these schools due to the negative environment around us or out of obedience to the Word of God? We must not assume that we are truly acting out of convictional obedience merely because we are doing the right thing.

Today's more modern brand of Christianity no longer stresses obedience or the commands and demands (fear) of God as the underlying cause of inspiration for our actions. It is not popular to talk in this kind of language. Our concept of God's love today is often far from Biblical, for it is an "easy believism" or "cheap grace."

It is popular now to consider God's Word as a book of "suggestions" and guidelines, and one in which God will bless you because of His grace, regardless of whether you obey Him or not. This kind of thinking is nonsense, for it mocks God's grace and true love, which are based and rooted in His law. His grace and love gives us the ability and desire to obey Him; it does not substitute for our obedience.

That is why it is important for parents and teachers to be fully convinced of what God's Word says about the training of their children. Without this, our foundation will not be strong enough to endure the test ahead. Let us now ponder some of the reasons why training our children consistently in Biblical truth as it relates to every area of life (every subject in the curriculum) is obedience to the Word of God and its commands.

Chapter 9
God's Law of Sowing and Reaping

Proverbs 22:6 Train up a child in the way he should go, And when he is old he will not depart from it.

Galatians 6:7-8 Do not be deceived, God is not mocked; for whatever a man sows, that he will also reap. [8] For he who sows to his flesh will of the flesh reap corruption, but he who sows to the Spirit will of the Spirit reap everlasting life.

Deuteronomy 22:9 "You shall not sow your vineyard with different kinds of seed, lest the yield of the seed which you have sown and the fruit of your vineyard be defiled.

Psalm 144:11-12 Rescue me and deliver me from the hand of foreigners, Whose mouth speaks lying words, And whose right hand is a right hand of falsehood-- [12] That our sons may be as plants grown up in their youth; That our daughters may be as pillars, Sculptured in palace style;

It is foolishness to "claim" the promise of Proverbs 22:6 simply because we have taken our children to church and Sunday school, and even given them good instruction at home, yet have allowed the world to sow a different seed into their minds for six hours a day, five days a week, and for over 13 years!

A child's thought patterns are formed through the disciplines of the academic subjects, and while we may teach concepts of Bible truth that conflict with these thought patterns at home, it will be the tendency and habit of our children to interpret all that we teach in light of humanistic principles. Unless the subjects and thought patterns that discipline the minds of our youth are Biblical, our children will have an unholy, carnal mind to deal with the rest of their lives.

Certainly God's grace can cover our mistakes and blind spots and produce renewal in our minds later on, yet we will still reap what we have sown, and the process later on in life will be much more difficult. God's grace is not an excuse for disobedience nor does it erase the consequences of sin. It is God's imputed favor that allows us free access and a relationship with Him that removes the eternal penalty of sin, but not its consequences. What is sown in the mind as thoughts will become actions and a lifestyle years later.

We must be consistent in the total planting process of training in order to expect a pure crop. Many argue that they have "turned out fine" graduating from non-Christian elementary or high school. The apparent "mixed seed" did not harm them, they declare.

However, the question is what is meant by "turning out fine?" Often, the very individuals who declare this in violation of God's Word profess Christianity while they practice humanism! When deceived, we are simply unaware of our inconsistency. The actual thought process of this argument, (rationalizing away a command of the Word), is fruit and evidence that the mixed seed planted while they were young had more affect than they realized.

The real issue is this: turning out fine according to God is being equipped to apply and live His Word in every area of life, learning God's viewpoint in all things. We mock God if we allow diverse seeds to be sown in our children. After all, weeds will grow on their own anyway. Does it make sense to plant them ourselves? If we sow seeds of life, and then plant seeds of death, only to expect a pure river of life, we mock one of God's bedrock principles! It is a natural and spiritual truth.

The character of one generation can only be correctly measured by the character of the next, and this generation's character of youth does not speak highly of our integrity or training. It is consistent training in God's Word from home, church, and school, that properly fits the context and meaning of Proverbs 22:6. This type of training, and godly instruction, can prevent us from raising and training "strange" children, who in their practice and lifestyle are strangers to the faith of God.

The way we are, with all of our hang-ups, is a result of the choices we have made based on the way we have been trained. We were either trained to defeat our old nature or feed upon it. The question is: what kind of platform of training will we give our children for the choices of their convictions? Let us not make the mistake other generations have made, and neglect the planting of proper seeds so the next generation can experience more of the glory of God than our own!

Maintaining an Equal Yoke Between Parent and Teacher

> **Amos 3:3** Can two walk together, unless they are agreed?
>
> **2 Corinthians 6:14** Do not be unequally yoked together with unbelievers. For what fellowship has righteousness with lawlessness? And what communion has light with darkness?
>
> **Luke 6:39-40** And He spoke a parable to them: "Can the blind lead the blind? Will they not both fall into the ditch? [40] A disciple is not above his teacher, but everyone who perfectly trained will be like his teacher.

We must see that our relationship as parent with the teacher that instructs our child is a yoke of covenant. Parents, and not the school or state, have been given the responsibility of overseeing the education of children (Ephesians 6:4); thus, they will be held responsible for those whom they allow to stand in their place and help train their children. If parents are ultimately accountable for the training of their children, then it stands to reason that next to the covenantal relationship between husband and wife, the strongest and tightest covenantal relationship is between parents (especially the father) and those who teach their children.

This is why home-schooling, particularly at the youngest ages, is such a safe and sound practice. Consistency is far easier to maintain when you are in covenant with yourself! It is evident that two cannot walk together adequately unless they are in agreement.

What should the parent and teacher agree upon? It should begin with the Lordship of Christ! Beginning with the authority of Scripture, agreement ideally should include the philosophy, principles, methodology, curriculum and administration of Christian education.

The teacher should set an example that the parent approves of as being a good influence upon their child. This does not mean being exactly like the parent, (for this is one of the advantages of working with others in the training of your children – to reveal and expose blind spots), but each should agree to hold in high esteem the Lordship of Jesus Christ, (Colossians 1:16-18). If not, then the parent is unequally yoked together with the teacher and is in disobedience with God's Word. Jesus clearly taught in Luke 6:39-40 that the disciple (or student) is not above his master (or teacher).

This means that it is foolishness to expect a child to rise above the teacher spiritually or morally, for maturity or the completion of a task (here translated perfection) is becoming like your teacher! Each parent must expect some of their own characteristics and mannerisms (both good and bad) to be seen in their children, yet the same holds true with teachers. Unless there is an equal yoke between parent and teacher, consistent training is impossible, for the child will have to choose which model to be like, and with the consistent help of his old nature, it may be the model that is closest to manifesting sinful traits, rather than godly character.

Parents are Responsible for What is Taught their Child

> **Proverbs 19:27** Cease listening to instruction, my son, And you will stray from the words of knowledge.
>
> **Matthew 18:6** "But whoever causes one of these little ones who believe in Me to sin, it would be better for him if a millstone were hung around his neck, and he were drowned in the depth of the sea.
>
> **James 3:1-2** My brethren, let not many of you become teachers, knowing that we shall receive a stricter judgment. [2] For we all stumble in many things. If anyone does not stumble in word, he is a perfect man, able also to bridle the whole body.

This third mandate or command, follows tight after the second. Jesus' words in Matthew 18:6 are very strong regarding the offending children. The word offense has an interesting meaning. The Greek transliteration in English is our word *scandalize*. It literally means "to entice to sin, or trap". It also means *"to bring shame."*

Webster begins his definition of scandal with the following remarks on the etymology of this word:

> "In Greek, this word signifies a stumbling-block, something against which a person impinges, or which causes him to fall … The primary sense of the root must be to drive, to thrust, or to strike or cast down."

He [Webster] goes on to say that its root is other languages embraces the concepts of confusion, dishonor, infamy, disfigure, spoil, violate, abuse, or defame.

How do these things happen to children? Is it just through physical abuse that a child is brought to shame of violation? Not at all, for this word comprehends everything that would cause a child to be offended or enticed to sin. It is sin that brings shame, violation, and dishonor, whether its attack is spiritual, mental or physical.

A child is born with a sinful nature but to entice a child to develop sinful spiritual practices (occult, evil, horror), intellectual practices (through patterns against the Word of God), and physical practices (violence, sexual perversion, etc.) is what Jesus says will bring the fierce judgment and wrath of Almighty God.

Parents are given the oversight of a child's education, and thus if they knowingly allow the teachers who stand in their place to teach things that would cause their child to stumble in any of these areas, they are guilty of the Lord's wrath. By definition, all secular education offends children, and only education that is according to Biblical principles will greatly reduce the amount of offense that comes their way.

A teacher's calling (translated "master" in James) is not a light thing. Here we are told that a teacher will receive greater judgment, for they are talking and teaching constantly. What a teacher teaches, the content and the attitude can either offend or bring life, for "death and life are in the power of the tongue", (Proverbs 18:21).

Parents, before God, must know what and how their children are being taught, since they are responsible for the training process. They will be held accountable and must be careful as to whom they delegate this responsibility.

An Ungodly Philosophy of Life Will Capture a Child's Mind

> **Jeremiah 10:2** Thus says the Lord: "Do not learn the way of the

Gentiles; Do not be dismayed at the signs of heaven, For the Gentiles are dismayed at them.

Colossians 2:8 Beware lest anyone cheat you through philosophy and empty deceit, according to the tradition of men, according to the basic principles of the world, and not according to Christ.

Romans 16:19 For your obedience has become known to all. Therefore I am glad on your behalf; but I want you to be wise in what is good, and simple concerning evil.

Isaiah 7:14-15 Therefore the Lord Himself will give you a sign: Behold, the virgin shall conceive and bear a Son, and shall call His name Immanuel. [15] Curds and honey He shall eat, that He may know to refuse the evil and choose the good.

Luke 2:51-52 Then He went down with them and came to Nazareth, and was subject to them, but His mother kept all these things in her heart. [52] And Jesus increased in wisdom and stature, and in favor with God and men.

Many Christians have been deceived into thinking that a "neutral" education is healthy for their child. Nothing could be further from the truth. In fact, there can be no such thing as a neutral education, because there is no such thing as neutral knowledge or a neutral child! All academic disciplines are interpreted by some value system based on religious presuppositions.

What the Scriptures clearly teach is that God does not want us to be taught a mixed or neutralized philosophy, for it will "trap" (translated "spoil" in Colossians 2:8) our minds. It is Satan who tries to trick and trap us by corrupting the mind (2nd Corinthians 11:3).

Christian education is a discipline of bringing every thought captive in obedience to Christ, (2 Corinthians 10:3-5). We are not to learn both the good (ways of Christ), and evil (ways of the devil and world) as if they were equal, so that we are knowledgeable in both. We must be taught that which is good as an absolute truth so that we can recognize that which is evil.

It is evident that in the life of Jesus, He was raised this way. We are told in Isaiah that He ate butter and honey (symbols of that which is pure and enlightens the eyes to see truth) in order to have the ability and habit of choosing the good.

Today, we think that we can allow all kinds of mixed seeds to be sown in both home and school, with our children becoming knowledgeable about evil, violence, and even the occult (through cartoons and other seemingly harmless activities) and still have them ready to serve the Lord. We must realize that they will be trapped in their minds if they learn the ways of the heathen. Our children need to be separated from the world before they will be able to minister to the world.

Children Should Be Taught About the Real World

> **Proverbs 1:7** The fear of the Lord is the beginning of knowledge, But fools despise wisdom and instruction.
>
> **Romans 11:36** For of Him and through Him and to Him are all things, to whom be glory forever. Amen.
>
> **2 Corinthians 4:18** while we do not look at the things which are seen, but at the things which are not seen. For the things which are seen are temporary, but the things which are not seen are eternal.
>
> **Colossians 1:17** And He is before all things, and in Him all things consist.

> **John 14:16** And I will pray the Father, and He will give you another Helper, that He may abide with you forever--

The *real world*, the *truth* about life, is found in Jesus, a person and not simply an ideology. He created all things, and all things were created to bear the stamp of the Godhead, (Romans 1:20). The fear, (or respect) of God is the foundation for knowledge, for Jesus Christ is the only foundation worth building upon, (1st Corinthians 3:11). When God is left out, it is a lie and the results are foolishness (see Romans 1:21-22).

A secular mind is literally one that is "worldly," a reprobate mind, (Romans 1:28). Christ is to have first place in all things for He is the one who holds the very universe together (Hebrews 1:1-3). The eternal things, (invisible, and attained in the spiritual realm) are to have priority over the temporal things (visible, and attained in the natural realm). We are not to lay up treasures on earth (temporal), but rather lay them up in things of eternal value (like our children), (see Matthew 6:19-20; and Corinthians 12:14).

When a child is trained by an educational system that denies, either blatantly, or through omission, that God is the ultimate reality in all things, then that child will grow up with the wrong priorities. At best it will be a mixture if his parents endeavor to teach him against what he has been taught. When intellectual achievement, athletics, and worldly success are continually placed before the child as the "real" world, we cannot help but reap corrupt behavior, thought patterns, and priorities.

The real world is where God reigns and is Sovereign, for that is, the only world that exists anyway. Thus, it is the parent who shelters his child from the real world if he withholds a Christian education from his children!

God's Ultimate Purpose for Youth

> **Psalm 127:3-5** Behold, children are a heritage from the Lord, The fruit of the womb is a reward.   [4] Like arrows in the hand of a warrior, So are the children of one's youth.   [5] Happy is the man who has his quiver full of them; They shall not be ashamed, But shall speak with their enemies in the gate.
>
> **Psalm 128:1-3** A Song of Ascents. Blessed is every one who fears the Lord, Who walks in His ways.   [2] When you eat the labor of your hands, You shall be happy, and it shall be well with you. [3] Your wife shall be like a fruitful vine In the very heart of your house, Your children like olive plants   All around your table.
>
> **Isaiah 58:12** Those from among you Shall build the old waste places; You shall raise up the foundations of many generations; And you shall be called the Repairer of the Breach, The Restorer of Streets to Dwell In.
>
> **2 Timothy 3:17** that the man of God may be complete, thoroughly equipped for every good work.

Often we are deceived as believers because we make *the starting line the finish line*. If God's ultimate purpose for our children was that they would be saved upon graduating from high school, then this might make Christian education merely an alternative worth pursuing when our teenagers are in trouble, (aside from the fact that it would still be in disobedience to the clear teaching of the Word of God). But God's goal is much more comprehensive than having youth get saved. He wants their education to be that part of their discipleship that teaches, exposes, reconstructs and helps them practice what to do as a result of their salvation, and how the Word of God brings solutions to every area of life.

Often we do not realize how mixed up we are. In the above Scriptures, God's call for youth as they enter adulthood (which is about 20 years of age from a Scriptural viewpoint) is to first be *arrows, or weapons of war,* understanding how to tear down enemy strongholds, or gates, and being unashamed at standing for truth. This implies an ability to reason, think, and stand for truth, discerning it from falsehood.

Youth are also called to be faithful like an olive tree. This means they will have the ability to produce solutions, not just remember what they have consumed.

Youth are called to help their parents and other adults rebuild and replace the fallen ruins of humanism with a true expression of Christian thought and practice. This is more involved than merely learning Sunday school lessons a few hours a week, or being involved in Bible studies. They need to know how to apply their Christianity to every area of life.

Youth are also called to be fully equipped to do every good work, and this comprehends seeing all of life from God's viewpoint, and understanding how every vocation can fit in with His plan.

The above ingredients are simply not possible if one must retrain young people after school hours and after their teen years. What is the point of having them learn the humanistic education while we desperately try to weed it out each night and weekend?

It denies us as parents and adults the opportunity to be on the same team with our teens while they are teenagers, enjoying some of the best of their lives and ours! It is a waste of valuable time and a mockery of God's grace when we are called to bring forth a harvest in their teen years.

Our vision has simply been too small and too low. Many have rejected Christian education because of this – and often what they have rejected is not true Christian education at all! If our goals are to have our youth saved by age 20, maybe we are on the right track.

But if God's goal is much more than this, a generation of youth willing to pay whatever the price necessary to see God's will established and having the ability to replace what sin has eroded, then we must raise the vision, standard, and goal, and pursue the right means of getting there.

Only with a proper foundation can we expect young people to fulfill their call of being that generation that God wishes to have arise in the earth as the standard against the flood of the enemy.

Chapter 10
Growing in Our Obedience

As the knowledge of God's commandments increase in our lives, we are responsible to it. This means that our obedience grows in its scope. We learn how to obey God in specific situations and in areas that affect our lives very practically. This section will address some of the ways in which we can do this in relation to the challenges that we face.

Settling Your Alternatives within a Biblical Framework

Once one knows what God requires, it is then necessary to adequately act upon that knowledge. This is what wisdom is all about. Being obedient does not mean being foolish, but it does mean that we realize what God requires. He will make a way for us to perform it (1st Thessalonians 5:24).

We must be willing to have God teach us, as well as willing to have His commands performed along the lines that He has ordained.

The Equally Yoked Family

> **James 4:17** Therefore, to him who knows to do good and does not do it, to him it is sin.

God holds a family accountable for what they know. Once a family understands God's commands and purposes, they are responsible to ask God for the grace, ability, and wisdom in carrying it out. For a family where both husband and wife are Christians, the simple response to God's command is obedience, full and complete. There is no excuse. It is important to recognize that disobedience is not an alternative in carrying out God's will! To refuse to do what God requires is sin.

A family must begin to plan and think within the only Biblical categories or alternatives given to them in the Word of God. Consider the following practical responses to Scriptural commands from an equally yoked family:

- Make a commitment to home school your children at least to age 5, so that a firm foundation can be laid in obedience to God's commands. It is more important to change your lifestyle than neglect the early education of your children by sending them to day care or preschools.

- Determine to send your children to a good Christian school when you wish to begin extending educational training to others.

- If there is no adequate Christian school, determine to home school your children as long as possible, and consider working to start a church school within your church if possible. If needed, employ good Christian tutors to help train your children.

- Before the Lord, ask Him for the grace within your life to make a covenant with your spouse never to direct your child to a secular school at least before college age in obedience to God's commands. Let this be known to your child, so that should he desire a secular school, the firm guidelines within Scriptural boundaries will have already been made. This brings greater security.

The Unequally Yoked Family

> **1 Corinthians 7:14** For the unbelieving husband is sanctified by the wife, and the unbelieving wife is sanctified by the husband; otherwise your children would be unclean, but now they are holy.

In the case of one parent being a believer and the other an unbeliever, God has a solution. The Scripture above was an answer to an unwritten but somewhat obvious question among believers at the time. The Old Testament had instructed mixed marriages at one time to get divorces since they had married in sin when uniting with strangers of the faith (see Ezra 10 and Nehemiah 13:23-29). The question must have been, what about marriages now where one has become a Christian and the other has not? Should we get divorces like they did in the Old Testament? The answer was the above Scripture passage.

The believing partner, by the grace extended through Christ, now sanctifies the unbelieving partner, and so divorce is both unnecessary and a greater sin for a believer to initiate. What does this have to do with obeying God in the education of our children?

Much in every way, for the Bible says that this sanctification includes the children. There is evidently an extra measure of grace in unequally yoked marriages in relation to children.

In pondering your response if you find yourself in this situation, consider the following:

- Endeavor to convince your unbelieving partner of the necessity of Christian education, appealing to reason when necessary to demonstrate the poor track record of government controlled and non-Christian education. Many will agree with the need when presented with the facts. Explore all options such as home-schooling, tutorial help, and an independent or church related Christian school.

- If you are the wife, ask God to give you the grace to submit to the decision of your husband and trust God that He will give you what is necessary to supplement their ungodly education. Do all you can to be educated yourself so that you are able to do this. You will probably end up home schooling your children "after hours" in some limited capacity. If possible, endeavor to gain from

Christian school teachers and parents the services and ministries available, even pondering the start of a "Sabbath school" on Saturdays or some sort of Sunday school that teaches more than devotions but applies the Word to other subjects.

- Seek the services of your church, especially if it operates a Christian school. If there is no ministry of Christian education that reaches out to those not in the school, start one with the right attitude. Also, seek to get your unbelieving spouse to be as active as possible in the church so he is exposed to the merits of Christian education, including programs and other activities put on by the school.

- If you are the husband, continue to gently lead as the head of your home, going as far as the submission and cooperation of your wife allows. Follow some of the same suggestions about wives listed above to help supplement what the child is obviously missing.

Remember, the key to winning an unbelieving husband is the submissive character of the wife, (see 1st Peter 3:1-6), and the key to winning an unbelieving wife is to honor her, (see 1st Peter 3:7).

The Broken Home

> **Psalm 68:6** God sets the solitary in families; He brings out those who are bound into prosperity; But the rebellious dwell in a dry land.

Often single parents, usually mothers, have quite a challenge obeying God in relation to Christian education. It is difficult for many to understand the loneliness and isolation felt by single mothers and fathers endeavoring to be both partners at once in fulfilling God's commands. There is no question that in these cases, God has ordained the complete natural family as well as the spiritual family of God to reach out and minister to the single parent and their children (See (James 1:27).

God has provided the context of the church through which the help can be organized and coordinated. The main need is sometimes financial due to the necessity of single parents working and fulfilling God's command to instruct and raise children. One thing is certain; help is essential. Consider some of the following suggestions:

- Seek out your own relatives first, and then within your church, for a family that you can trust and that you might be honest with in discussing your situation. Don't be artificial, for this relationship may develop over time and take you quite a while to establish.

- Although churches should initiate this kind of ministry, they often do not, and completed families (husband and wife together) are usually unaware of the plight of the widow, divorced, and/or single parent, usually with fatherless children. In God's grace, you must seek out help from a family you are drawn to.

- If you cannot do this with a family in your church, search in your immediate neighborhood, but be careful not to become unequally yoked with an unbelieving family (2 Corinthians 6:14). Endeavor to be honest with this family involving your financial needs, child care assistance needs and even child discipline and relations with a former husband, etc. Ideally, a kind of covenant can be formed where they will help you and work with you – for God sets the solitary (or lonely) in (relation to) families (Psalm 68:6a).

You must guard against several attitudes and actions that will bring you into disobedience with God's Word. Do not think you are incapable of independence because you seek help from others. God has ordained it this way. Do not allow yourself to become, on the other hand, too dependent upon the family that assists you – you and this family must be honest about the fact that what you need is help to become independent and yet vitally related to them at the same time!

Ask God for the grace needed from Him to remain pure before Him. Pray for the ability to be independent financially, or receive local financial assistance (from individual families, a small home fellowship, your local church or Christian school), but avoid state welfare. God will honor your obedience to His Word in trusting His Divine institutions of home and church to meet your needs rather than trusting in Caesar (or the State).

Seek God for the strength to train up your children in the way that they should be trained, and avoid sending them to pre schools or day care centers. Seek help from families and those described above for this kind of assistance in child care and training.

How Long Should a Child Receive a Christian Education?

> **Galatians 4:1-2** Now I say that the heir, as long as he is a child, does not differ at all from a slave, though he is master of all, [2] but is under guardians and stewards until the time appointed by the father.

Here Paul the apostle uses the analogy of education within a home to illustrate his later application of our sonship in Christ. For our purposes now, his analogy is helpful.

The heir is the child, or son, who will probably inherit much later on. However, as long as he is a child (and the word indicates younger than 20 years of age) he differs nothing from a servant even though he eventually will be an adult. A child is under the tutors and governors (teachers allowed to teach him) as long as the father (who is responsible for education) determines it is necessary (beyond age 20).

From this we can deduce the following:

- A child should receive a Christian education at least through what is now determined to be the high school years, not fully becoming an adult until around 20, (see Numbers 1:3 and following for an indication that an adult was one "numbered twenty years and upward").

- Beyond this, the father, or family and elders of the church in covenant with a single mother, need to discern whether the child needs to have Christian education continued or is prepared to battle the challenges of humanistic ideologies on his own. Some children mature earlier, and some later, and so the father should determine when Christian education is no longer needed, or in other words, the child is not in need of further close tutoring under the eyes of the father from a strictly Christian point of view.

- When making decisions about college, all must remember that the purpose of training is to equip people to fulfill God's call and thus a secular education is often inadequate at the college level as well. Also, age 20 usually covers most of the college years. However, the difficulty in finding a college of this kind of quality is understandable.

Many great mistakes are made when families feel that the high school years are the years that a child least needs a Christian education. This is because of this stage youth are refining their skills of applying Christianity, and it is simply not possible for those who do not know the Lord to properly harvest the gifts and potential of a student. Needless to say, those that stop the Christian education of their child at 12 or 13 are in disobedience to the Word of God.

What about the Will of the Child?

> **Isaiah 7:14-15** Therefore the Lord Himself will give you a sign: Behold, the virgin shall conceive and bear a Son, and shall call His name Immanuel. [15] Curds and honey He shall eat, that He may know to refuse the evil and choose the good.

Another challenge involves the child or student who does not want a Christian education, either initially or most commonly in the teen years. If we are obedient to God in properly training our children, the great majority of them will freely choose to continue their education like Jesus did at age 12. Before age 12, it should be the parent's choice anyway. If good seeds are down early, they will sprout later on.

In the teen years, everything that has been planted will come up; you can count on it! Jesus was taught the pure (butter and honey) that he might later voluntarily choose to do what is right. Since none of us are perfect, and none of us have children like Jesus, we face obvious challenges and the ideal escapes us.

God knows this, and His grace is available at all times to give us the ability to follow His Word and gain the results He has promised. The Christian high school has a calling that is deeper than baby sitting stubborn children who do not want to be there.

It is the time of harvest. If what one seems to be harvesting are weeds, a little leaven will leaven the whole lump (1st Corinthians 5:6-7). One rotten attitude within a teenager spreads like wildfire and will poison the vision of excellence within a school!

It does not take much to water down a vision of excellence to one of mediocrity and a lukewarm spiritual atmosphere. Everyone suffers in this kind of environment.

Like church discipline, the rebellious child must be confronted individually, then with several (even students can be involved here at the teen level), and eventually with parents and elders if it goes that far. If there is still no submission, then expulsion from school (and at times to secular schooling) is potentially allowing the civil government to punish the prodigal, (see Deuteronomy 21:18-21 and Luke 15:15).

Ponder some of these suggestions:

- Before 12, the child should be obedient to the parent's choice in receiving a Christian education. The parent's will is not questioned, and we work in school with all children by parental commitment unless the child rebels and deserves to be excommunicated from the school.

- From about age 12, or usually the 7th grade, both the conviction of the parents and the child needs to be sought. We have each fill out separate applications, and interview both separately. From age 12 on upward, the heart and will of the child needs to be more involved in taking responsibility and initiative in the continuation of his or her Christian education.

- If the child does not wish to receive the training in the school at any age, proper steps must be followed with the family involving school officials and the elders of the church. This must be done to determine the potential faults in parents with respect to balanced child training practices, as well as provide an atmosphere and environment to restore the proper attitude in the child. It is the home that is responsible to seek for a correction in the attitude of the child, and this could include the option of removing the child from school, but teaching them at home, or even the relocation of the child to another home within the church for a more successful time of reformation.

- If this proves unsuccessful, then expulsion is necessary. Like church discipline, all the steps must be followed, and expulsion form school must be treated as serious as church discipline. The reason we must treat expulsion as a parallel to church discipline is because the child is stubbornly remaining in sin if he refuses to submit to the legitimate discipline of his parents. Children under 20 are still under their parents jurisdiction (and remain so even if expelled from the school, as long as they are living under their roof), but the child has forsaken the spiritual covering of his parents, which is very serious. There is always hope with the grace of God, but in order to obey Him we cannot allow the scorner to spoil those who remain. This becomes quite a challenge when the parents are the ones who wish to remove the child. However, if the parents are covenanted members of a church, they should be confronted and dealt with in a similar order regarding their decision.

Home School or Christian School?

Colossians 3:20-21 Children, obey your parents in all things, for this is well pleasing to the Lord. [21] Fathers, do not provoke your children, lest they become discouraged.

As we have stated previously, the home is the key foundation for all of education. All of education begins with the right of the parent to rule and the right of the child to obey. The father is given specific responsibility to determine the direction, oversight, and duration of schooling.

Just as the father determines the duration of educational instruction within the home, so he should also determine who teaches his children (Galatians 4:1-2). The Biblical model of education seems to combine both home schooling and institutional (private or church) schooling. The only type of institutional schooling taught in God's Word is a direct extension of the family (like tutors), or the local church.

The Bible does not seem to present a model of either sole parental instruction or sole institutional instruction.

Consider some of the following suggestions:

- The foundation of all education, at least up to age 5 (Kindergarten year) should be within the home. This should be the rule and not the exception. It is during this time when the security and loyalty is laid within a child in relation to his parents. This is essential when entering a group or team later on.

- In grades K-3, or ages 5-8, home schooling is recommended for establishing and confirming virtue within the child that can only come through direct relationships with parents. During these grades the ideal set up is for a combined home and Christian school where the child is taught at home but attends some classes at school specified by the parent. At times, even a single parent may wish to home school with another family they are in covenant with as mentioned before. Most often, however, they may utilize the Christian school entirely.

- In grades 4-6, or ages 9-11, home schooling becomes more of an option related to specific cases than the general rule. However, it is imperative that parents discern potential flaws in character development at this time, for it is still a very precious time to home school in order to build and/or correct character. Counsel with teachers, elders and other parents is often helpful to get a good appraisal of a child's character development at this point.

- In grades 7-12, or ages 12-18, the Christian school often provides what teens need most and cannot be given at home – team ministry in the context of the local church. Home school should be more of an exception here. However, if a child has not had the opportunity to build personal relationships with his parents, or there is a special need, home school may still be viable and necessary.

Restoring the Parents as the Primary Educators

In summary, we could make the following points about the need for parents to obey God and His commands.

- Obedience is the most important response for homes. We must learn what God requires, and expect His love to cause us to desire to obey.

- We should settle in our minds that the disciplining of our children in every area of life is as much a part of our Christian faith as any other, producing a conviction that will not change no matter what the cost.

- The Word of God must become central in establishing this conviction so that we stand on firm ground, persuaded in our minds and able and willing to persuade others. We need to make decisions by dealing with all challenges in the context of obedience rather than compromising our faith.

- We must also grow in our obedience to God by purging our homes of hindrances that reduce our effectiveness in training our children. Our children need to grow up in an atmosphere where God's priorities and standards are elevated to honor His eternal purposes.

- Finally, we must restore the parental role to that of primary educator. We must remain active and involved in the education of our children even after we extend this task to others.

Dr. Bernier's books include:

- *Shades of Gray: Discerning the Standard of Christian Ethics*
- *Powerful Living*
- *Fruitful Living*
- *Rise Up and Build: Transforming Principles in the Life and Ministry of Nehemiah.*
- *Principles & Practice of the Pastoral Ministry*
- *Christian Foundations*

For more information contact:

Master Builder Ministries, Inc.
397 Bay Street
Fall River, Massachusetts 02724
(508) 730-1735
www.mbministries.org

or

Vision Publishing

1-800-9-VISION

www.visionpublishingservices.com

www.ingramcontent.com/pod-product-compliance
Lightning Source LLC
Chambersburg PA
CBHW060846050426
42453CB00008B/854